Pure Brightness Shines Everywhere

The Glass of China

The Sage-Saint absorbs the absolute (Dao)
thus reflecting and illuminating (Ying) the world

Zong Bing (375–443)

Pure Brightness Shines Everywhere

The Glass of China

Edited by Emily Byrne Curtis
with essays by Ricardo Joppert, Ph.D., Ma Wenkuan, and Daphne Lange Rosenzweig, Ph.D.

ASHGATE

Published by

Ashgate Publishing Limited	Ashgate Publishing Company
Gower House	Suite 420
Croft Road	101 Cherry Street
Aldershot	Burlington
Hants GU11 3HR	Vermont, 05401-4405
England	USA

Ashgate website: http://www.ashgate.com

British Library Cataloguing in Publication Data

Pure Brightness Shines Everywhere: The Glass of China
    1. Glassware – China – History.   2. Glass manufacture – China – History.
    I. Curtis, Emily Byrne
    748.2′9951

US Library of Congress Cataloging in Publication Data

Pure Brightness Shines Everywhere: The Glass of China / edited by Emily Byrne
    Curtis, with essays by Ricardo Joppert, Ma Wenkuan, and Daphne Lange
    Rosenzweig.
        p.   cm.
    Includes bibliographical references and index.
    1. Glassware – China.   I. Curtis, Emily Byrne.   II. Joppert, Ricardo.
    III. Wenkuan, Ma.   IV. Rosenzweig, Daphne 1941–
    NK5183.A1G58 2003
    748.2′0951–dc22   2003057842

ISBN 0 7546 0981 2

This book is printed on acid free paper.

Typeset by Graphicraft Ltd., Hong Kong

Printed and bound in Singapore

Contents

WITHDRAWN

List of Illustrations

Contributors

Ricardo Joppert, Ph.D.
Director
Museu Itamaraty
Rio de Janeiro
Brazil

Ma Wenkuan
Institute of Archaeology
Chinese Academy for Social Sciences
Beijing
China

Daphne Lange Rosenzweig, Ph.D.
Liberal Arts Program
Ringling School of Art and Design
Sarasota, Florida
USA

Acknowledgments

Since it took many years for this book to move from the its original inspiration to full completion, there are many individuals and institutions to whom I owe my thanks. I should like to acknowledge first the contributions of the collaborating authors: Ricardo Joppert, Ma Wenkuan, and Daphne Lange Rosenzweig, for the interesting and diverse perspectives they have given to the subject of Chinese glass.

A considerable portion of source material for the book was obtained directly from the many archives and libraries of Rome which my husband and I visited time and again during the last decade. Two of these should be singled out for special recognition: The archive of de Propaganda Fide and the Jesuit Archive (ARSI). At Archivum de Propaganda Fide we thank the generous and professional assistance of Archivist Giovanni Fosci, and at ARSI, the friendly cooperation of Wiktor Gramatowski, S. J., and his successor Joseph DeCock, S. J. Research was conducted with the aid of the International Chinese Snuff Bottle Society, and a grant from the Pacific Cultural Foundation, Taiwan.

Another treasure trove of documents awaited us at the Congrégation de la Mission in Paris, where Paul Henzmann, C. M. was instrumental in our finding material, not only relevant to our subject, but which also illuminated the background. Brigitte Appavou, at the Archives des Missions Etrangères provided further assistance and encouragement.

I wish to acknowledge my debt to John Finlay for his translation of the Chinese plan of the glassworks, and to Hugh Moss for kindly providing me with an advance copy of his glass chronology, which was most helpful. Special mention should be made of Archivist Louis Derbes, C. M. I wish also to thank William Lillyman for obtaining a copy of the *Dongchao chongyang lu*, and Pamela Edwardes, who found a very able and thoughtful reader to help me improve my manuscript.

The New York Public Library's knowledgeable and patient staff is due particular mention, and I am extremely grateful for the illustrations which have been generously provided by private collectors.

Throughout the project's duration, colleagues and friends have provided inspiration and assistance. I thank them all, and many others too numerous to name.

As usual my husband, Myron, was my first editor and critic, and has modified my prose, clarified my thought, and given me his unstinting support.

The faults in this work are mine and many a precision and a grace will be theirs.

Preface

To consider an entire book devoted to the subject of Chinese glass, long considered a minor art by some authorities on the Middle Kingdom, would have in times past seemed a limited and fruitless task. Until recently, lack of sufficient documentation or even interest would have deterred the most ardent of devotees from tackling this fascinating subject. Throughout the last century various authors have allotted in their works some space for discussion of the subject, drawing on sparse documentation combined with educated speculation. A great deal of this information has turned out to be correct, and some of it left in question. Of the works on the subject of Chinese glass, a few have stood as standard references for those who might need supporting material when considering related arts. Stephen Bushell's *Chinese Art*, London 1909; W. B. Honey's *Chinese Glass*, and John Ayers' (1964) 'Chinese Glass' in *Transactions of the Oriental Ceramic Society*, and 'Later Chinese Glass', *Journal of Glass Studies*, (1977) by Phelps Warren are perhaps most often quoted.

The more recent surge of interest in Chinese glass seems to have commenced with an exhibition of the Clague collection at the Phoenix Art Museum in 1987, and carried to spectacular heights with an exhibition of Chinese glass at the China House Gallery, New York in 1990. It is interesting to note that the catalogue for the latter, began to lean, for the first time, more heavily on western missionary sources for material relating to Qing dynasty glass, perhaps the most productive and some would consider the most interesting period of Chinese glass. Concurrent with these events this author, propelled by independent inspiration and motivation, obtained grants for research on the subject in Rome.

This approach was spawned from an intriguing passage in John Bell's *A Journey from St Petersburg to Peking* concerning 'the Emperor's glass-house, which his Imperial Majesty often visits with pleasure. . . . The person employed to superintend and carry on this design was Kilian Stumpff [sic], a German father, lately deceased, a man in great favour with the Emperor, and well known, in China, for his ingenuity and literature.' This is the first time that the name Kilian Stumpf had surfaced in other than specialized ecclesiastical literature and the question had to be asked, just what did Stumpf and his European successors do and how did it effect the course of Chinese glassmaking?

Unlikely as it may theretofore have seemed, it seemed clear that answers to these and other questions were to be found in the archives in Rome and other places in Europe. The quest for documentation took me to Rome and Paris several times in the last decade where each time, another intriguing bit of the puzzle would reveal itself. A case in point is the discovery of the Chinese plan for the Imperial glass workshop established by the missionaries within the confines of the Imperial city. This document cemented the disparate mosaic of data pointing to the infusion of European glassmaking techniques into China and silenced, somewhat, the perennial nay-sayers in this regard. Carrying this methodology forward, this author has attempted to correlate the hitherto unpublished or little known documents from these archives with the vast amount of material in the Palace Museum, Beijing.

I am fortunate to have secured the collaboration of associate scholars whose insights and experience in the field of Chinese art breathe into the text a broad sense of how Chinese glass in its physical aspect draws from other cultural influences and how it relates to the traditional Chinese world view. Daphne Lange Rosenzweig has illuminated the connections between Chinese glass and ancient traditional forms. Ricardo Joppert has given us a powerful linkage between Chinese philosophical tenets and the properties of glass, and Ma Wenkuan in turn has probed the study of excavated specimens and the influences of Islamic glass on its Chinese counterpart.

This author has considered at length the problem of the dating of Chinese glass in general and that of the pieces illustrated in this book in particular. This is particularly troublesome with regard to Qing dynasty glass. The conclusion has been reached to take the conservative route and designate to the period only those pieces whose provenance has been corroborated by either continuous ownership or verified chronological lineage. For the other examples whose form, style and appearance strongly suggest a specific period, I have on the side of caution, prefaced many of the descriptions with the phrase 'attributed to.'

Although there is certainly more to be revealed in the history of glassmaking in China, it is hoped that this book in its scope, makes clear some of the basic facts of its development and proves engaging in its reading. We also hope that this work will stimulate further studies by local historians, museum curators, art historians, and collectors.

Chronology

SHANG		*c.*1500–1028 BC	
ZHOU		1028–256 BC	
Warring States		480–221 BC	
QIN		221–206 BC	
HAN		206 BC–AD 220	
THE SIX DYNASTIES		221–581	
SUI		581–618	
TANG		618–906	
THE FIVE DYNASTIES		907–60	
SONG		960–1279	
Northern Song		960–1127	
Southern Song		1128–1279	
JIN		1115–1234	
YUAN		1260–1368	

MING		1368–1644	
Hongwu	1368–98	Hongzhi	1488–1505
Jianwen	1399–1402	Zhengde	1506–21
Yongle	1403–24	Jiajing	1522–66
Hongxi	1425	Longqing	1567–72
Xuande	1426–35	Wanli	1573–1619
Zhengtong	1436–49	Taichang	1620
Jingtai	1450–57	Tianqi	1621–27
Taishun	1457–64	Congzhen	1628–44
Chenghua	1465–87		

QING		1644–1912	
Shunzi	1644–61	Daoguang	1821–50
Kangxi	1662–1722	Xianfeng	1851–61
Yongzheng	1723–35	Tongzhi	1862–74
Qianlong	1736–95	Guangxu	1875–1908
Jiaqing	1796–1820	Xuantong	1909–11

REPUBLIC	1912–

Abbreviations

Abbreviation	Full reference
Archives	First National Historical Archive of China (*Zhongguo diyi lishi dang'anguan*)
APF	Archivum S. Congregationis de Propaganda Fide
ARSI	Archivum Romanum Societatis Iesu

1

Form and Ritual in Chinese Glass

Daphne Lange Rosenzweig, Ph.D.

Every ritual in China was associated with a well-defined performance act, in which participants were engaged in prescribed verbal recitations, musical passages, and body movements, which together with appropriate ritual implements, created a total ritual 'package'.

Diverse in intent, Chinese rituals impacted and involved all levels of society, from Shanghai courtesans (whose 'micro-rituals', held within their houses of prostitution, celebrated the 'Birthdays of the God of Wealth')[1] to emperors (whose exalted status required them to preside over the state 'macro-rituals' held at the Altars of Heaven, Earth, Sun, and Moon).[2] Intended to 'clarify and impose obligations', rituals possessed both cosmological and social significance.[3] Though the internal significance of many rituals (such as the Buddhist Water and Land Ritual, performed to save all sentient beings from hell)[4] might have eluded casual viewers and even enactors, nevertheless they were performed as part of the traditional obligations associated with their social or religious group.

Some rituals were specific to (and could only be led by) a person in a certain position (the emperor or empress, eldest son, new bride, etc). Such rituals defined major familial life passages (such as capping, marriage, death)[5] or signaled nationally important moments in the annual agricultural and sericultural cycles. Other rituals of regional importance, such as veneration of the city god, would be celebrated by larger, more socially diverse groups. Guilds had rituals, women's quarters had rituals, farmers had rituals. No aspect of life was without its associative rituals.

No matter what the intended purpose of the ritual or the status of the performers, altars, altar garniture sets, and other objects of ritual practice were essential as ceremonial focal points and conveyors of offerings. It is these objects and their forms with which we are concerned in this brief essay.

Surviving Chinese glass artifacts fall into several distinct categories. They encompass objects for personal adornment, containers and other utensils, scholar's table and cabinet objects, and ritual objects, including altar furniture. The types vary by period. Glass cicadas for placing on the tongues of the deceased, glass pigs for burial, even glass *bi* 璧, are clearly more popular in earlier periods, whereas

1.1 Belt hooks, center example cast in the form of two coiling animals with three swirled glass beads, l 18.5 cm (7¹/₄ in.), gilt-bronze, Late Warring States period (8th–2nd century BC), Roger Keverne Ltd

snuff bottles, larger ritual-form vases, and even items such as plate glass for green-houses[6] are clearly products of later workshops.

A variety of inspirations for Chinese glass forms and designs have been identified. One of the most important was the desire to imitate the ancient, or *fang gu* 仿古, as illustrated here by the Warring States period (Late Zhou) gilt-bronze belt hooks (see Fig. 1.1) and the golden yellow glass belt hook from the Qing dynasty, (see Fig. 1.2). Though seen from above, the bronze hooks have the same overall shape and animal decor as the glass and, interestingly, the central belt hook has three swirled glass beads.

1.2 Belt hook, golden yellow, carved and pierced with a *chilong*-head terminal gazing upon another one next to the top, l 10.2 cm (4 in.), glass, 18th–19th century, coll. William Lillyman

1.3 Ming sacrificial altar, for Imperial rituals, stone, Beijing, coll. Daphne Rosenzweig

Although ritual objects of Shang, Zhou and Han were integral to Chinese cultural consciousness, avidly collected by later connoisseurs and illustrated in numerous woodblock print volumes, it is the Song and Ming interpretations of the classic forms which often had a more direct influence on later Chinese glass production. Interestingly, one author has suggested that the attenuated forms of mid and late Qing vessels, including vases and ritual types, may not be so much a taste of the times or a desire to alter an established style for the sake of freshness, but the unintended result of distortions published in poorly printed woodblock manuals.[7]

Another source of inspiration for glass was the desire to imitate natural materials, which was perhaps less an artistic imperative than a commercially desirable factor. Though a variety of materials were imitated successfully in glass, the colors and textural marks of jades, other hardstones, and precious stones, were considered particularly desirable, and appear in ritual objects. A third and highly important influence on Chinese glass (though of less importance for ritual vessels) was imported forms.

Identifying forms and designs unique to, or first created in, glass is difficult. Even during the mid-Qing period, when glass snuff bottle creation blossomed, and a plethora of other glass types was produced, designs often were reliant on other media. A series of attractive Qing glass and jade table screens for the scholar's studio, for example, are redolent of the aura of Song, Yuan and Ming painting. Not surprisingly, these 'Pictorial Style' design sources are often paintings in the palace collections;[8] it is possible that workshop artisans were allowed to view such works. Though records fail to verify visits of workshop artisans to the painting storage, there are documented links between earlier and later court paintings.[9] The conservatism of later Chinese glass ritual vessels is not an isolated trait; it exists in other aspects of the artistic culture of Qing and pre-Qing periods.

A question to consider is this: was glass ever an essential part of Chinese ritual performance and what was its practicality as a material for a functional ritual vessel? Modern authors have addressed themselves primarily to the terminology, chemistry and dating of glass, the import–export trade in glass, the history of glass workshop production, including identification of individual hands, and the aesthetics of individual objects from published collections. When it comes to the designation of glass objects as having been created for ritual purposes, however, it is often unclear how they would have functioned in actual performances. Their practicality as containers for foods or wines or for incense burning has also to be determined. Were they of (and technically could they have been created in) the size requisite for public performance of the ritual (see Fig. 1.3) where large scale would be important to the extended audience's perception of the ritual's efficacy? Were they of a scale more suitable for private rituals, on domestic altars?

A fascinating area of glass history yet to be explored is the association of glass with Daoist rites. The late Han Daoist movement called 'Way of the Celestial

Masters' (highly influential through the tenth century) espoused the elimination of animal and food sacrifices. No form of sacrifice was allowed; theoretically this eliminated the use of altar ritual vessels. Since the *boshanlu* 博山爐 (hill censer) form of incense burner was particularly popular in the Han, the extent to which this was practised is unclear; ritual vessels (particularly the *ding* 鼎 tripod which, when lidded, was used as a censer) were a prominent, indeed, essential part of Daoist ritual performances. The censer 'symbolizes the gate between the human world and the realm of the gods'.[10] Few identifiably Daoist incense burners exist from pre-Ming times, but there are extant Ming and Qing examples.

Links between Daoism and glass could be a fertile area for investigation, since glass so suitably expresses principles of Daoist philosophy. The elusiveness of the sheen, as a viewer moves in relation to a glass object, the reflective transformation as the visible becomes invisible (or the reverse), the 'nothingness' of clarity – all these characteristics should mean that glass was the perfect manufactured material (analogous to clear quartz, the natural material) for Daoist practice. Research into Daoist texts and scrolls illustrating Daoist rituals, together with identification and examination of Daoist grave sites, should clarify whether this perceived desirability of glass 'power' objects and containers can be confirmed archivally and archaeologically.[11]

Certainly Buddhist practice utilized precious materials for altar and ash containers and incense burners, but while illustrations in paintings or woodblock prints readily convey the shapes of ritual vessels, they are less informative about the materials of those vessels. It is difficult to discern when (and if) the medium of glass may have been involved. However, numerous eighteenth century Buddhist gilt votive objects in the collections of the National Palace Museum, Taipei, include decorative glass inserts.[12]

The traditional *ding* tripod form, in its evolved Eastern Zhou rounded contour form with small pot belly and out-turned splayed legs, appears repeatedly in actual censers (incense burners) associated with Buddhist temple sites. Two works, illustrated here, indicate the close formal relationship between bronze and glass in these censers. The Tang silvered-bronze jar with cover (see Fig. 1.4), and a rare, amethyst glass incense burner and cover (see Fig. 1.5), dated to the Qianlong period were probably created for use on smaller altars. The decor of the glass is more elaborate, but the forms are essentially identical, indicating the evolution of design and retention of shape so characteristic of the *fang gu* movement.

In one of the Lamaist temples associated with the Imperial court of the Qing, there is (or was) a set of twelve glass *ding* vessels, used to hold incense, as evidenced by remaining incense ashes. The glass appears in twelve different tones, imitating hardstone materials. While it is true that these glass vessels were intended for use, some of the remaining works from this now scattered set still retain the bronze inserts with gilded designs which enabled them to function in the first instance; clearly it was deemed essential to have a hardy liner of another

1.4 Jar and cover with bud-shaped knop, supported on three cabriole legs, h 17.1 cm (6³/₄ in.), silvered-bronze, Tang dynasty (618–906), Roger Keverne Ltd

1.5 Incense burner and cover, transparent amethyst, carved with two panels, each with a dragon chasing a pearl, h 14 cm (5¹/₂ in.), glass, Qianlong period (1736–95), Roger Keverne Ltd

1.6 Chimera paper weight or brush rest, its 'fang gu' form derived from Han jade examples, l 11.5 cm (4⁵/₈ in.), clear glass, *c.*1800, private coll.

material for purposes of safety and functionality. Their size is such that they must have been intended for private, not public purposes. Their twelve colors compel us to think of Chinese color theory.

Extensive research has been done into the colors of early and later Chinese glass,[13] but more is essential, because color is one of the main components of a variety of systems which attempt to identify the forces of the universe. For example, in the Daoist Way of the Celestial Masters, there are Three Heavens, one each representing Mystery, Principle and Origin. The three colors of blue, yellow, and white were associated with this system, which also represents Heaven, Earth and Water. Would Daoist ritual objects for altars engaged in the Way of the Celestial Masters be fitted out with blue, yellow and white ritual vessels? Would city temples and house altars, directionally located, reflect the azure associated with the east, vermilion of the south, white of the west, and black of the north? The Altar of Land and Grain, site of an Imperial sacrifice, was 'constructed out of soil in the colours of the five directions, which was brought from every corner of the empire'; would its sacrificial vessels appear in the five colors?[14] Would colors associated with the cycle of twelve years each be dominant on altars for that particular year? Are the rich yolk yellows, bright yellows, orange yellows, golden yellows, and tawny yellows, assigned to specific ranks at court, actually achieved in art works? The answer to this apparently would be 'yes', at least in the realm of porcelain and textiles; but did glass technicians have the palette control to reflect rank? Are those large, inscribed, yellow glass vases which appear so often at auction and in private collections definable as a specific yellow from amongst these subtly differentiated descriptions?[15]

Properly performed rituals are a prominent factor in Chinese cultural history. Extended research into the objects employed in the actual performances, the suitability of glass for such objects, and the potentially significant relationship between glass colors and deities, directions, cycles, and religious affiliations, should prove a useful supplement to current knowledge of the ritual performance package.

NOTES
The author would like to acknowledge the assistance of the International Center for Eastern Archaeology & Cultural History, Boston University, in preparation for this paper.

1. Yeh (1988), pp. 43, 49
2. Shan Guoqiang *et al.* (1990), p. 76
3. Robins (2001), pp. 1153
4. Little *et al.* (2000), pp. 28, 227
5. Watson and Ravoski (1988), p. 3
6. Matire, p. 48
7. Michaelson (2000), pp. 4–7
8. Chang Li-tuan (1997), pp. 51–2, 189–209 #24
9. Rosenzweig (1991)
10. Little *et al.* (2000), note 4, pp. 41, 137, 189, and p. 218 #2
11. Yang Boda (1991), p. 137
12. National Palace Museum (1995)
13. Lawson (1997), p. 179
14. Shan Guoqiang *et al.* (1990), note 2, p. 76
15. Mehlman (1983), #14

2.1a Kneeling figure, h 1.4 cm (⁵/₈ in.), faience, Early Warring States period, 5th century BC, coll. Simon Kwan

2.1b Reverse of 2.1a

2

Chinese Glass Technology

There are many reasons for plumbing the scientific nature of glass not the least of which is to illuminate the physical properties of the material itself, in order to give insight into the problems of glassmakers throughout history. As an aid to the art historian, it has been thought that such a study might lead to some scheme for the categorizing of glass pieces with regard to date and locale of origin. In some cases it has been possible to do so, but with the glass of China such definitive determinations elude us. From the earliest times Chinese glass has exhibited a varied composition reflecting the disparate sources of raw materials, and complicated by the occasional mingling of western glass in the manufacturing process. Although it is not possible to establish the uniqueness of Chinese glass from a chemical standpoint, several analyses shed light on its various components and provide us with a timeline for its evolution.

The earliest studies on the composition of Chinese glass were conducted in the 1930s, studies by C. G. Seligman and H. C. Beck. They were the first to note that a very high proportion of lead (PbO) was contained in Chinese glass of early periods and some also contained unusually high concentrations of barium oxide (BaO).[1] High concentrations of these compounds, and a combination of the two, have been verified in recent studies of the chemistry of glasses in which a variety of pieces of early provenance were examined along with other historic glasses from all over the world. The results have been published in *Chemical Analyses of Early Glasses* by Robert H. Brill and John H. Martin and have relevance mainly in reference to early glass.[2] Chinese glass of later periods does not exhibit these properties.

It will be helpful to reiterate a few of the fundamentals of glass. At its most basic level, glass is a substance composed of silica and a flux such as soda (Na_2Co_2) or potash (K_2O). Since the silica which is usually obtained in the form of quartz melts at such a high temperature the flux is added to reduce the melting temperature. To the above is added lime (CaO) which makes the mix less soluble in water. These basic ingredients are present to varying degrees in the great variety of glasses we encounter throughout history. In addition, various other compounds either by chance or intent are present in trace amounts to give glass its aesthetic qualities, such as color and translucency.[3] For practical purposes virtually all ancient glass is of the soda-lime-silica variety. (Soda (Na_2O) was the predominant alkali in glass until the medieval period, when potash (K_2O) came into use.)[4]

Some scholars argue that early Western Zhou (10th–9th centuries BC) glass, which consists of bonded polycrystalline quartz beads resembling glass, is not actually glass. The tombs of the Earl of Yu 伯與 and his consort Jing Ji 井姬, at Rujiazhuang village in the Baoji district, yielded light blue round and cylindrical beads, as well as strings made up of agate pieces, and handle-shaped jades with glass inlays. There were also kernel-shaped glass pieces with pointed ends. The surface of the latter pieces was covered with stippled protuberances, enhancing the decorative effect.[5] Since the chemical compositions of the beads are dominated by SiO_2, and there are large amounts of crystalline quartz present, strictly speaking, this material should not be called glass, but instead faience, as found in other parts of the world. But the sword decorations are of transparent glass, generally calcium-silicate glass (CaO-SiO_2) or potassium-calcium-silicate glass (K_2O-CaO-SiO_2).

The shapes of the round and cylindrical glass beads indicate a definite influence from jade and stone working, and Western Zhou glass is probably the first glass made in imitation of jade. This imitation was intended to replicate the shape, significance, and luster of jades — a major distinctive feature of Chinese glass, and also one of the distinguishing marks between Chinese and western glassware. The barium heretofore referred to could have been introduced intentionally as a separate ingredient, because it produced a certain turbidity in the glasses which might have been regarded as desirable by early Chinese glassmakers since it gave the glasses a jade-like appearance. On the other hand, the barium could have performed either the fluxing function of alkali or the stabilizing function of lime.

Small and exquisite glass objects (see Fig. 2.2) have often been found in the tombs of the Spring and Autumn period (770–476 BC) and the Warring States period (475–221 BC). The earliest of these objects are two double-handled cups and a plate. The technique and composition of these glass vessels followed the established tradition of the Warring States period, that is, they were made of lead-barium glass. In 1977, archaeologists of the Yangzhou Museum unearthed a tomb dating to the late Western Han dynasty (206 BC–AD 24). Within was a lady of noble rank named Mo Shu 莫叔, covered with a 'glass garment' — a sort of adornment for the head or body — and consisting of about six hundred pieces of glass of different sizes and shapes, including rectangles, trapezoids, and circles. The round pieces and a few of the rectangular ones have surface decorations of hydras, flowers, and plants, while other pieces have undecorated surfaces. It is believed that all of the glass garment pieces were mold-pressed. They were probably formed by placing crushed glass in a mold and heating it in a furnace or kiln.[6]

As to color, by the fourth year (113 BC) of the Wudi 元帝 Emperor, Chinese artisans had already produced an emerald colored glass tray and a glass *yushang*

2.2 Cup, weathered white, decorated with raised nipple pattern, h 8 cm (3¹/₈ in.), glass, Warring States period (480–221BC), Zache Auktionen Wien, 27 March, 1999, #41

2.3 Miniature bowl, weathered brownish with incised flower, d 2.8 cm (1¹/₄ in.), glass, Han dynasty, (206BC–AD220), coll. Alan E. Feen

羽觴 cup or 'feather-handled cup'. Qualitative spectrochemical analysis determined that the main raw materials used to make the glass tray were silicon and lead, but that it also contained sodium and barium. Japanese scholars believe that the ingredients used to make the tray and the cup were placed in a stone or pottery mold, which was allowed to cool when the object had taken shape; the object was then ground and polished to attain its final appearance. This technique was similar to the nineteenth century French one of *patê-de-verre*.[7] The green of Chinese lead glasses is due to the presence of copper and iron, but there are also some opaque white, amber, violet-blue, red, and dark brown glasses, indicating that during this historical period Chinese craftsmen had mastered the art of glass coloring.[8] A fluorescent x-ray and microscopic investigation, conducted by Corning, of one axe head (see Fig. 2.4) revealed that its pale emerald tone is due to the presence of small amounts of iron and copper, and that the composition of the glass is 45 per cent lead (PbO) with no barium (BaO). While we can only speculate on the actual use for a glass axe head, its relationship similarly decorated to jade and bronze ones of earlier periods is quite evident.[9]

Chinese archaeology has now provided a good number of eyebeads (see Fig. 2.6) for analysis and study.[10] Such beads excavated from a late Spring and Autumn tomb in Gushi county, Henan province, are K-Ca glass and it is possible that they

13

2.4 Axe head of translucent green color with relief carving, h 3.5 cm (1⅝ in.), glass, Han dynasty (206BC–AD220), coll. Alan E. Feen

2.5 Cups in chrysanthemum shape, clear white, h 2.7 cm (1⅛ in.), glass, late Tang to Northern Song (9th–11th century), coll. Simon Kwan

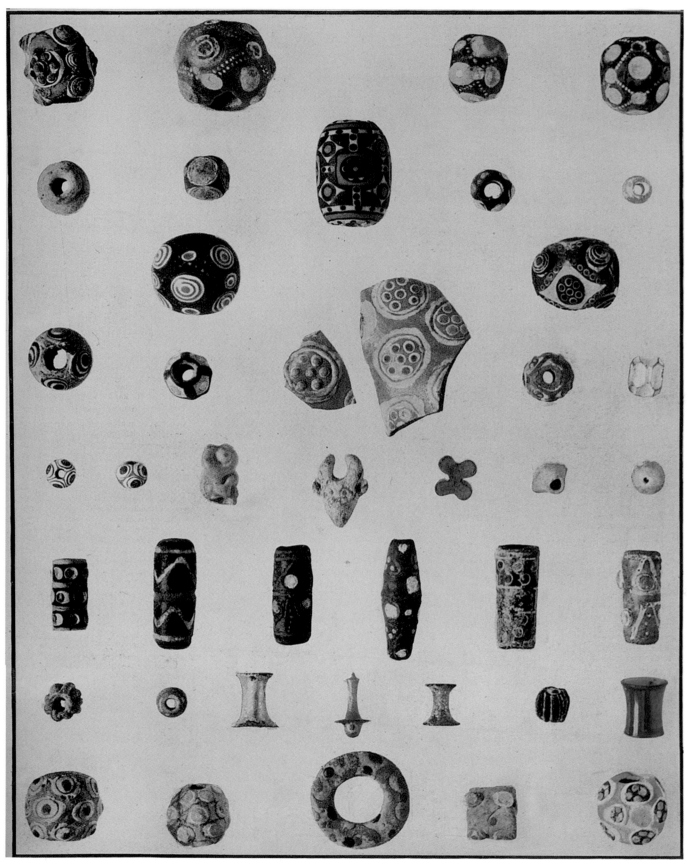

2.6 Tubes, eye beads, and ear studs, glass and faience, Warring States (480–221BC), plate from *The Illustrated London News*, 5 May 1934

were imports from beyond China. Tests of eyebeads from other tombs determined that they were made of Pb-Ba glass, which was different from the K-Ca glass prevalent in the West at the same time. Chinese and western scholars have subsequently agreed that the Pb-Ca glass is indeed native to China. Eyebeads were highly decorative and the workmanship required to make them is comparatively complex; from damaged beads we know that in the manufacturing process an elliptical trench was first made on the rough cast, and then several layers of spherical colored pieces of glass were inlaid to form the eyes.

It is believed that glassblowing was invented in the Middle East, perhaps in Syria, about 50–25 BC. In China, however, glassblowing did not develop until later. The gourd-shaped bottles, vase, calabash, and monk's alms bowl found in a Northern Wei (386–534) stupa at Jingxian, Hebei province, are the most important glass vessels retrieved from that period. All of them were blown. This was an important turning point in the history of Chinese glassmaking, because it made mass production possible and glass products less expensive. The bottles themselves, have a round lip formed by an inward rolling of the mouth and trailed-on feet. These techniques were passed down from the Roman and Sasanian traditions, but the forms of the vessels are traditional Chinese ones, and pottery of similar shapes can be found in China.

Many fine glass vessels have been discovered from the Sui dynasty (581–618). Analysis of glass objects from the tomb of Li Jingxun 李靜訓 in Xi'an indicated that the making of soda-lime glass and the use of the pontil began in China at this time. The fashioning of glass funerary garment pieces, *bi* discs, lances and belt hooks, gradually disappeared and two tendencies became evident: conceptual innovation which led artisans to shift focus over time from depicting the supernatural to the human and natural world, and technological advancement which occurred as glass craftsmen sought the most appropriate manner in which to give form to their conceptions.

From the Tang (618–907) to the Yuan (1271–1368) dynasties, the glassware uncovered consists mostly of small free-blown reliquary vessels. The most outstanding Tang glass vessels, are the two yellow vases, a green cup, and a green bottle unearthed in a tomb in Yunxian, Hubei province. Chemical analysis of fragments showed that the glass contains a high percentage of lead (64 per cent PbO), and that the vessels were blown, with the mouth fire-polished to form the lip. Written records inform us that glass hair clasps were produced in the Tang dynasty, and that in the Song dynasty (960–1279) the majority of women were wearing hair ornaments made from glass. A southern Song poem contains the following couplet: 'When in the capital they prohibited pearls and jade; The empire was filled with glass.' We may surmise from this that glass hair ornaments were attractive and inexpensive, which put them within the purchasing power of the urban masses.[11]

Some examples of rings and hairpins in opaque off-white or turquoise glass may be products of the glassworks in Zibo, Shandong. Excavation of this site

2.7 Ingot, dark blue with surface iridescence, base with incised mark, h 7.6 cm
(2⁷/₈ in.), glass, probably Ming dynasty (1368–1644), coll. Philip C. Cardeiro

revealed the foundations of twenty furnace pits which are believed to date to the
time between the late Yuan and early Ming periods. Glass beads, hair clasps, and
ornaments together with the remains of clay pots and waste glass were gathered as
samples for testing. It was determined that pieces of well-melted blue opal waste
glass owed their 'blue vitriol' color to the coloring effects of the cupric ion, and
their opalescence to the presence of CaF_2 crystals (see Fig. 2.7). Further investiga-
tions showed that a secondary process had been employed to fashion the hairpins,
that is, glass rods or tubes had been reheated and then reformed. Button-like
ornaments were made by reheating and molding. These artifacts confirmed the use
of various forming techniques at the ancient glassworks.[12]

Qing dynasty (1644–1912) glass deserves an important place in the history of
Chinese glass. Under the patronage of Qing rulers many new varieties of glass
were made, and it was an outstanding period of artistic accomplishment. K_2O and
PbO, which were used as fluxes in ancient Chinese glass preceding the Qing
dynasty, proved to be also the main fluxes of the glass analyzed by Shi Meiguang
and Zhou Fenzheng samples from the Palace Museum, Beijing (see Fig. 2.8). The
raw glass materials used by the Imperial workshops included 'horse-tooth stone',
saltpeter, borax, white arsenic, and fluorspar. The saltpeter referred to should be
potassium nitrate, which was used also as a raw material in the fourteenth century
potash-lime glass in Boshan. According to Shi and Zhou's findings, the MgO
content of the glass made from the saltpeter was very low (below 0.5 per cent),
while the MgO content of western medieval glasses made from plant ash was

17

much higher (more than 3–5 per cent). 'Horse-tooth stone' could be feldspar. Qing glassmaking was influenced by western technology because some glasses contained B_2O_3 and As_2O_3, which were introduced as borax and white arsenic, respectively.[13] The colorants included oxides of copper, iron, and cobalt. Spectral analysis showed that the red glass on the cameo samples contained a small amount (about 0.01 per cent) of gold. Gold ruby glass can be made when there is colloidal gold present at this level. The red color is caused by selective light scattering of the gold particles in the glass.

It is now believed that the composition for most of the red glass vessels in the museum's collection from the Yongzheng 雍正 (r.1723–35) and Qianlong 乾隆 (r.1736–95) reigns were gold-derived. This appears in the palace records as *lianghong* 亮紅. Furthermore, an inventory made in 1752 of the materials used in the Imperial glassworks recorded the presence of 'three *liang* 兩 of top quality gold leaf for mixing with glass.'[14] This technology was successfully transferred from the court to Boshan by 1820, and made its way to Guangzhou 廣州 (Canton), as evidenced by an observation made in 1875 where:

> In order to make red glass, the workman mixes with the ingredients, which we have already enumerated, a certain quantity of gold leaf. Artificial flowers also, with which the Chinese decorate their ancestral and public altars, and which are made of thin copper, and coated with gold leaf, are, when old, and, therefore, no longer required, not unfrequently bought by glass blowers, and, for this very purpose, used.[15]

Thus strengthened, glass artisans were able to withstand the loss of Imperial patronage, and continue on into the twentieth century. Present day craftsmen are busily producing art glass in the Chinese tradition using modern technology. The age old methods in the handling and working of the molten material, however, remain the same, and in the hands of the artist.

NOTES

1. See, *Nature* (1934), vol. 133, no 6, p. 982 and (1936), vol. 38, p. 721
2. Brill and Martin (eds) (1991), pp. 31–42
3. Brill (1963), pp. 120–31
4. Brill (1968), p. 48
5. Yang Boda (1998), no pagination
6. Brill and Martin (eds) (1991), pp. 21, 34, 48
7. Yang Boda (1998)
8. Brill and Martin (eds) (1991), p. 27
9. Private correspondence, also Curtis (1998), pp. 98–9, and Fig. 1
10. These beads are currently referred to in China as 'dragon fly eyes' (*qingting yan*)
11. Brill and Martin (eds) (1991), pp. 7–8, and Yang Boda (1998)
12. Yi Jialiang and Tu Shulin, in Brill (1991), pp. 99–101
13. Shi Meiguang and Zhou Fuzheng (1993), pp. 102–105
14. Zhang Weiyong (2000), p. 75
15. Gray (1875), p. 239

Below are the results of a study by Shi Meiguang and Zhou Fuzheng exclusively of Qing Dynasty glass which used pieces from the Palace Museum.. Using the methods of X-ray fluorescence supported by X-ray diffraction and other technologies, the following data emerged:

Specimen	SiO_2	Al_2O_3	CaO	MgO	PbO	K_2O	Na_2O	Fe_2O_3	CuO	B_2O_3	Other Oxides	Density g/cm³	Method*
1- Fragment of Cameo Vessel	65.48	0.15	2.05	0.07	5.96	14.62	2.60	0.05		2.79	As_2O =3.17	2.538	ICP
2- Fragment of imitation jadeite glass 2	38.65	0.43			44.74	9.59	0.32	0.61	0.37		SnO=1.80	3.77	ICP
3- Fragment of Cameo Vessel 3	64.91	0.54	2.03	0.13	4.57	15.34	3.90	0.11		2.59	As_2O_3 = 2.28	2.512	ICP
4- Red glass 4	65.52	0.32	2.04	0.07	4.57	14.41	4.44	0.12		2.36	As_2O_3 = 2.45		ICP
5- Fragment of vase handle 5	66.53	1.03	1.85	0.02	4.86	15.78	3.87	0.25	0.02	2.05	CoO = 0.18	2.533	AAS
6- Wall fragment of Cup	74.80	1.63	0.19	0.04		20.89	0.18	0.15	0.49			2.385	AAS
7- Wall fragment of faceted snuff bottle	67.74	0.80	5.61	0.09		21.76	0.42	0.37					AAS
8- Neck fragment of faceted snuff bottle	65.91	1.95	6.73	0.13		22.50		0.42	0.25		CoO = 0.075	2.453	AAS
9- Glass petal	60.57	5.66	12.39	2.21		12.76	3.88	0.48				2.520	AAS
10- Flat glass	69.80	1.22	14.10	0.09	0.25	0.28	11.98	0.29				2.561	AAS
11- Wall fragment of thin-walled blown bowl	42.44	0.08	0.03		38.57	14.54	0.19	0.09					ICP
12- glass rod	56.21		6.31		14.35	23.11							EDX
13- Weathered surface layer of previous specimen	70.32	1.86	8.04		18.34	1.44							EDX

1 - Qianlong period (1736-1796); white opaque cases with red, thickness 4.6 mm.
2 - Probably 18th century; turbid green.
3 - 18th century; red on white, sample has white opaque under-layer, thickness 4-5 mm.
4 - Removed from previous specimen, spectral analysis reveals approximately 0.01% gold.
5 - 18th century; blue opaque, thickness 6 mm.
6 - 18th century; green transparent.
7 - 18th century; amber transparent, thickness 1.2 - 2.3 mm.
8 - 18th century; bleu transparent.
9 - 18th century; white opaque.
10 - 19th century; greenish transparent, thickness 2.3 mm.
11 - 18th-19th century; colorless, thickness 1.1 mm.
12 - 19th century; colorless, weathered and eroded, diameter 3 mm.
13 - Weathered surface layer of specimen # 12.

*Method: ICP - Inductively coupled plasma emission spectrometry (ICP-ES)
AAS - Atomic absorption spectrometry
EDX - Dispersive X-ray fluorescence

2.8 Results of chemical analyses conducted by Shi Meiguang and Zhou Fuzheng

3

Glass Properties as Metaphors for Wisdom in China

Ricardo Joppert, Ph.D.

Transparency has always been a vital need for the Chinese mind. It was first looked for by people during the Neolithic period in the morphology of the veins of stones, as the only right way (*dao* 道) to polish them in order to provide an useful instrument for daily life. Later, mental evolution led the Chinese to see in the transparency of jade a good metaphor for their search in the higher levels of existence: jade is such a special stone that its morphology predestinates it to a certain shape; otherwise it will break. So, as with events in life, all have an 'internal logic' (*li*), which is the key for success or failure. This concept is expressed in the *Daxue* (大學 *Great Learning*) as, 'Extension of knowledge (*zhi zhi* 至知) depends on the investigation of things (*gewu* 格物)... things being invest-igated (*wuge*), knowledge becomes complete (*zhizhi*).'[1]

The transparent qualities of jade have naturally led to research concerning glass. Historical texts tell us that western glassmaking technology was being learned by the Chinese as early as the Qin dynasty (221–206 BC),[2] and some extraordinary glass objects imitating jade ritual implements, such as the *bi* 璧 ring (the symbol of heaven) and the *yue* 鉞 axes (see Figs. 3.1 and 3.2), have been dated to the Han dynasty. These are evidence that in early times glass played a role analogous to jade in ancestor worship (still alive in our modern times), which, of course, evokes a cohesion between the living and the dead in China's organic thought, prevailing even beyond death itself: the 'internal logic' (*li*) shown through transparency means, therefore, absolute unity.

For the Chinese the universe is an organic whole: diversity leads to unity and destinies follow a way (*dao*) which is absolute order (*li* 理). When the heart rests in equanimity (*ping* 平) this order can be reflected (*zhao* 照) in individual destinies which themselves will be illuminative (*zhao*) of the absolute way.

Zhuang Zhou 莊周, the presumed author of the book now known as the Zhuangzi, also called the *Nanhua Zhen Jing* 南華真經 (*True Book of Nanhua*) frequently used three metaphors in connection with transparency and spiritual

3.1 *Bi* disk with carved grain pattern, weathered greenish white, d 18.3 cm (5³/₈ in.), glass, Han dynasty (206BC–AD220), Zacke Auktionen Wien, 27 March 1999, #43

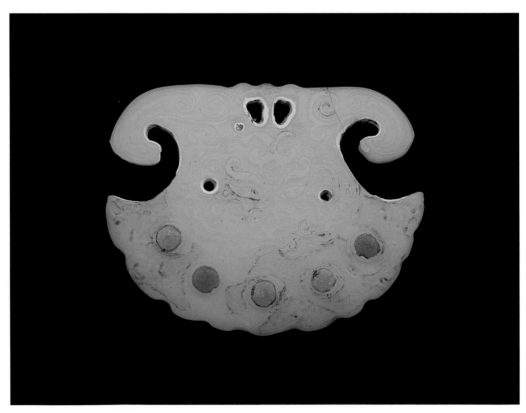

3.2 Pendant in form of axe head with relief carving and turquoise inlays, white, h 5 cm (2 in.), glass, probably Tang dynasty (618–906), private coll.

achievement: those of the reflection of light, the mirror and water. For instance, in order to fulfil its mission of active reflection, the surface – of water, for instance – must remain unruffled, as in Zhuang's metaphor for the heart of the sage (or saint – *sheng* 聖): 'when the surface of the heart is calm, it is like the essential enlightened spirit (*jing shen* 精神): the heart of the sage should remain in tranquility (*jing* 靜) – it will be the mirror (*jian* 鑑) of the universe, it will reflect (*jing* 鏡) the multitude of beings.'[3]

Some Chinese words are intimately linked to the idea of reflection: *zhao* 照, *ming* 明, and *ying* 映, for example. In Chinese ideography all carry in common the radicals of either 'fire' (*huo*) or 'sun' (*ri*), which convey the general idea and crystalize them as vectors of *yang*, the positive energy of the cosmos.

But, in Chinese, 'reflection' means 'full illumination'. Thus a reflection must always arise in its object the consciousness or the assertion of its own existence: in the word *ming* ('brightness') – in which the graphs for 'sun' and 'moon' are conjugated – the evidence of the sun is completed by its reflection over the lunar surface. In the philosophical sense, such is the function of gnosis ('spiritual knowledge').

The mirror, water and the quiet reflection that they can induce are therefore metaphors for one's heart in its fundamental state (*ben xing* 本性) of 'non-disturbance'. These are Daoist ideas, their metaphor for heaven in man: 'the mirror and the water, in their contact with forms, have no need for intellection; this notwithstanding, nothing eludes them: neither square angularities, nor round aspects; neither curves, nor straight lines . . . ; likewise it is not by happenstance that the echo always responds to sounds: its self-sufficiency is a result of its passivity (*moran* 默然) . . . man is born without agitation (*jing*) – it is heavens's nature in him (*tian zhi xing* 天之性) – through commotion (*gan* 感) however his nature is disturbed (*dong* 動) and deteriorates (*hai* 害); his spirit responds to things and intellection is put into motion . . . in this way, the natural internal logic (*tian li* 天理) is destroyed.'[4]

Light and radiance have of course been objects of speculation to philosophers in many cultures, as with Buddhism, which was introduced to China from India, in the first century BC. But it took a long time for this new religion to have some significance in the country, since China, though not closed to foreign ideas, always adapts them before accepting an alien creed. In many ways, Buddhism had to borrow from native Daoism, including modifying the metaphor of the image of the mirror according to its own principles (the image had antecedents in India).

By the Tang dynasty, Buddhism had attained full maturity in the new land. The mid-eighth century 'Platform *Sûtra* of the Sixth Patriarch' (*Tanjing* 壇經 – a work which heralded sudden enlightenment (*dun wu*) in Chan (Japanese Zen) Buddhism – denies the possibility of analogy between a mirror (to be dusted) and the nature of man (to be purified). This nature is pure from the outset; it has no form: 'the pure mirror has no stand' (*ming jing yi wu tai*) and therefore no room for dust – by sudden insight alone is Buddhahood attained.

The metaphoric qualities of glass began to be exploited – for instance, the transformation of this material into a jade simulant. This was perfect for Buddhist *Mahâyâna* theory, which admits that the Buddha has in fact 'Three Bodies' (*Trikâya*): *Dharmakâya* – the 'Body of the Law', the Absolute which encompasses all; *Sambhogakâya* – the 'Body of Joy', a state of bliss, a mystical body which appears to the *Bodhisattva*(s) in extasis only; the *Nirmânakâya* – the 'Body of Metamorphosis', the one poor mortals see; a projection in the world of the above-mentioned ones.

Like in the alchemy of cinnabar or gold – preconized in Daoism – glass symbolizes all these transformations, due to its peculiar characteristics. But one essence only is maintained. Glass bowls inside reliquaries began to be used to contain the ashes of the holy ones (*sarîra* in Sanskrit; *sheli* 舍利 in Chinese), after cremation: another symbol for metamorphosis, as they represented the supermundane and indestructible knowledge of the Body of Transformation, now deceased.[5] Extraordinary examples of these reliquaries have been unearthed in the Famensi 法門寺 pagoda, Shaanxi, and in the Temple of the Great Clouds (Dayunsi 大雲寺), Gansu.

Buddhism in China belongs to the *Mahâyâna* schism ('Greater Vehicle of Illumination'), which had evolved from primitive Buddhism, the so-called *Hînayâna* ('Lesser Vehicle') – or *Theravada* ('Words of the Ancients') – Buddhism, which prevails in SouthEast Asia. The *Theravada* sects are *exoteric*, local and limited; with the *Mahâyâna*, Buddhism becomes *esoteric* and aims at the universal. *Nirvâna* (extinction of the self) is the purpose of the *Theravada*; salvation of all beings and omniscience, that of the *Mahâyâna*. A new figure appears: that of the *Bodhisattva*, a being who, although capable of entering *Nirvâna*, restrains from doing so, in order to help beings (see Fig. 3.4). Iconographically speaking, the historical *Sâkyamuni* (*Nirmânakâya*) Buddha, having entered *Nirvâna*, is represented dressed in a monk's robe without any adornment. The *Bodhisattva*, on the other hand, who chooses to remain in the world, wears worldly attributes, such as jewels. Jewelry becomes symbolic in some *Mahâyâna* texts, and translucency and radiance were viewed as metaphors for the highest virtues, as emphasized in the '*Sûtra* of the Garland of flowers' (Sansc.: *AVATAMSAKASÛTRA*; Chin. *HUAYANJING* 華嚴經), which became highly influential in Tang China. It was patronized by a usurper, Empress Wu Zetian 武則天 (Wu Zhao 648–704).

For the *Avatamsaka*, everything in the world is interfused and the origin of all is the *Dharmakâya* Body of the Buddha. For this reason, this *sûtra* admits manifestation of infinite *Nirmânakâya* (metamorphic) Buddha(s) or visions of them. All of them radiate light. And being metamorphic, in the way glass can be, these emanations do not loose their link with Essential *Dharmakâya*. Thus, *Dharmakâya* should be conceived not only as the Absolute Truth of the Universe, but also as the universe itself in its multiple aspects. *Dharmâkâya*, the 'Body of Brightness', stands alone, (*zhao ti du li* 照體獨立).

Certain Buddhist schools linked to Xuan Zang 玄奘, the pilgrim, acknowledge *Âdarshajñana* – 'mirror wisdom' – a faculty of omniscience inherent to the Buddha(s), through which everything that can be known reflects itself in their spirit: this wisdom can be transmitted to people, thus shining through the Buddha(s) to them. Probably, the best iconographic example of this is the enormous Tang dynasty *Rocana* (the 'Light') Buddha (675) at the Longmen caves near Luoyang – in front of which one may experience the intuition of one's own destiny, as if reflected in the eyes of the statue.

This being the case, one understands why glass properties – such as transformation, purity, transparency – became natural metaphors, whose material support became the mirror and the jewels which the *Bodhisattva*(s) iconographically wear. In this sense, gems are equaled to the ashes (*sarîra*, *sheli*) resulting from the cremation of the holy men, indeed of the historical Buddha himself, for these ashes are also the result of metamorphosis. Being connected to one's fundamental nature, to diversity within unity, to mutation without loss of Essence, they finally lead to a state of repose and quietism without which true and full spiritual consciousness cannot be achieved.

3.3 'A Thousand Eyes', clear pale yellow, h 31 cm (12¹/₈ in.), glass, sculpture by Heinrich Wang, *Be joyful and At Ease: Heinrich Wang Glass Art Exhibition, 1999*

Glass and glass connected arts have continued to be prized by the Chinese today, although no longer directly reflecting the religious symbolism of former times. Like an echo of those ancient spiritual values, glass properties were often viewed, after the Tang dynasty, in the light of aesthetics. Some very interesting glass objects have been published from the Ming dynasty. And, of course, during the last, (alien) Manchu, Qing dynasty 'traditional Chinese technology was allied, through western missionaries, to European innovations; under (Manchu) patronage, Chinese glassmaking experienced a period of unprecedented development.'[6]

Under this aesthetic spell – which reflects (*zhao*) unconscious religious values – glass art forms are being revitalized in Taiwan by Heinrich Wang (Wang Xiajun 王俠軍), who has been creating exquisite pieces which provide a fresh interpretation of Chinese traditional designs (see Fig. 3.3).

Symbolic verses in which the great Tang poet Wang Wei 王維,[7] describes the imagery of a lump of ice melting down inside a vessel of transparent jade seem an appropriate close to this essay, as they speak of this quietism which is the reflection (*zhao*) of the Absolute:

Brightness is contained within,

But the interior veils no mystery;

Purity is self-enclosed,

But from the outside it seems to be empty.

(抱明中不隱

Bao ming zhong bu yin

含淨外疑虛

Han jing wai yi xu)

('Pure like ice inside a jade vessel')

Written at the age of nineteen (718)

NOTES

1. *Daxue* (trans. J. Legge, *Great Learning*), ch. 1
2. Curtis (1998), pp. 98–9
3. Nanhua – a place where the famous thinker would have sojourned, see Guo Xiang, *Zhuang zi* (or *Nanhua Zhen Jing*), ch. 1
4. Liu An 劉安, *Huainanzi*, ch. '*Yuan dao*' (Return to the Original Way)
5. Berger (1997), p. 67
6. Curtis (1998), p. 100
7. Wang Wei (699–759), became famous both as a poet and painter
8. '*Qing Ru Yu Hu Bing* 清如玉壺冰', (*Imperial Approved: Complete Tang Poems*), Guangxu-Dinghai, 1887

26

3.4 Seated figure of the *Bodhisattva* Guanyin, h 20 cm (7⁷/₈ in.), glass simulating crystal, 19th century, coll. Alan E. Feen

4

Islamic Glass Unearthed in China

Ma Wenkuan

馬文寬

In the second year of the Tang dynasty emperor Gaozong's Yonghui reign (AD 651), the Arab empire established diplomatic relations with China. From then on, contact was frequent, trade was rapidly developed, and fine Islamic glass was imported into China. Sima Guang recorded in his *Comprehensive Mirror for Aid in Government* (*Zi Tongjian* 資治通鑑) that in AD 775, Lu Sigong, governor of the Lingnan region under the Tang dynasty, had plundered glass dishes (ca.27–30 cm in diameter) from overseas traders in Guangzhou and presented them to the prime minister and the emperor. This indicates that large Islamic glass dishes were already imported into China in the second half of the eighth century and regarded as valuable treasures. According to the *History of the Song*: 'Foreign Countries' (*Songshi: Waiguo Chuan* 宋史: 外國傳) in the fourth year of Dazhong Xiangfu reign (AD 1011), *Tazi*, i.e. the Arab empire, offered the Song emperor Zhenzong 'bluish-white glass wine vessels' as tribute. Both of the textual records have been verified by the archaeological excavations carried out in recent decades.

Islamic glass has been recovered from four Tang period sites:

1. In 1987, the crypt of the pagoda at Famen temple in Fufeng county, Shaanxi province, yielded a batch of glass. It included four dishes with incised design, two dishes with gilded incised design (see Fig. 4.1), one dish decorated in enamel (see Fig. 4.2), two cylindrical cups with mold-impressed design (see Fig. 4.3) and one dish-mouthed vase with applied pattern.[1] The pagoda was built in the first year of the Tang Qianfu reign (AD 874). So this glass can be dated to a period earlier than the middle of the ninth century, even as early as the second half of the eighth century. These items must have been produced in Mesopotamia as their designs are largely identical with those popular there. Some scholars believe that the glass dishes from the Famen temple are products from Nishapur in eastern Iran, based on the fact that counterparts were unearthed in that city. This view is incorrect. Nishapur in the ninth and tenth centuries was merely a local political and military center. Although it was famous for the production of pottery at that time, it was unable to produce exquisite

4.1 Dish, transparent turquoise blue with glided incised design, d 15.7 cm (6¼ in.), glass, excavated from crypt sealed in 874, 8th–9th century

4.2 Dish, decorated in luster, d 14.1 cm (5½ in.), glass, excavated from crypt sealed in 874, 8th–9th century

4.3 Cup, weathered clear with mold-impressed design, h 8.4 cm (3¹/₄ in.), glass, excavated from crypt sealed in 874, 8th–9th century

luster painted and tin-glazed blue-and-white pottery, let alone glass of so high a quality. The excellent glass found at Nishapur must also have been imported from Mesopotamia.

2. In 1969, the crypt of the pagoda at the Jingzhi temple in Dingxian county, Hebei province, yielded two cylindrical cups (one blue the other white), two narrow-necked vases (see Fig. 4.4) and a small square vase. The pagoda was first constructed in the second year of the Xing'an reign, Northern Wei period (AD 453) and rebuilt four times, in the Sui, Tang and Song dynasties. According to the 'Inscription of the Rebuilding of the Sâkyamuni Sarîra Stupa at the Jingzhi Temple' and the 'record of the Reburial of Buddha's Relics at the Jingzhi Temple of Tang Dynasty Dingzhou District', this Islamic glass should be dated to the ninth century.[2]

3. No. 188 Tang tomb at Guanlin in Luoyang city yielded a bottle with a short narrow neck.[3] A counterpart of the vessel was among the cultural relics plundered from Luoyang by the Canadian Bishop W. C. White.[4] Both objects must be scent-sprinklers and date from the eighth–ninth century.

4. In 1990–1991, more than two hundred glass fragments were unearthed from the ruins of a late Tang building in Yangzhou, which may have been the remains of the 'residence-cum-store' of a trader from the western regions. The original forms cannot be reconstructed,[5] but according to the report of their scientific tests, the fragments are certainly Islamic glass.[6]

4.4 Vase, transparent brownish with speckles, h 7.1 cm (2⅝ in.), glass, excavated from crypt of a stupa dated to 9th century

One site contained Islamic glass of the Five Dynasties period:

In 1981, the Min king's tomb excavated in the suburbs of Fuzhou city, Fujian province, yielded fragments of Islamic glass. The tomb dates from AD 932.[7]

Three sites yielded Islamic glass from the Song period:

1. The above mentioned crypt of the pagoda at Jingzhi temple in Dingxian county yielded, in addition, a narrow-necked glass vase with incised design and a dark blue glass scent-sprinkler (see Fig. 4.5), which belong to the Islamic glassware of the tenth century. As the crypt was sealed in AD 977, the two vessels can be dated to the middle of the tenth century or earlier.[8]

2. In 1971, the ruined Sarîra Stupa in Wuwei county, Anhui province, yielded a narrow-necked vase with incised design (see Fig. 4.6). It is identical in shape and decoration to those unearthed from the crypt of the pagoda at the Jingzhi temple in Dingzhou district.[9] The stupa was built in AD 1036.

3. In 1966–7, the Huiguang pagoda in Rui'an county of Zhejiang province yielded a dish-mouthed ball-bellied narrow-necked glass vase with incised design (see Fig. 4.7). The pagoda was built in AD 1043.[10]

4.5 Scent-sprinkler, dark blue, h 18 cm (7 in.), glass, excavated from a Northern Song stupa sealed in 977, 9th–10th century

4.6 Vase, transparent with incised design, h 9.8 cm (3³/₄ in.), excavated from the crypt of a stupa dated to mid-tenth century

4.7 Vase, transparent with long neck and engraved design, h 9 cm (3¹/₂ in.), glass, excavated from a Northern Song stupa built in 1043

Islamic glassware was recovered from Liao period tombs and pagodas, at six sites:

1. In 1954, a Liao tomb in Chifeng City, Inner Mongolia, yielded fragments of a small-mouthed glass vase. The tomb goes back to AD 959.[11]

2. In 1974, an early Liao tomb at Yemoutai in Faku county, Liaoning province, yielded a square green glass condiment vessel.[12] The vessel is similar to the yellowish-green glazed square pottery condiment vessel in the British Museum, London. The latter bears the Arabic inscription 'The work of Abu Nasr of Basra in Egypt.'[13] Thus, the glass condiment vessel must be a product made in the Islamic domains of either Iraq or Egypt.

3. In 1986, a Liao tomb in Naiman banner, Inner Mongolia, yielded a dish-mouthed narrow-necked vase with incised design, two-handled plain cups (see Fig. 4.8), a handled cup with cut design, a dish with cut design in relief (see Fig. 4.9) and two high-necked vases. The tomb dates from AD 1018.[14]

4.8 Cup, dark green with handle, h 11.4 cm (4¹/₂ in.), glass, excavated from a Liao tomb dated AD1018

4.9 Dish, iridescent with cut relief design, d 25.5 cm (10 in.), glass, excavated from a
Liao tomb dated AD1018

4.10 Ewer, clear with handle and enclosed
savîra, h 16 cm (6¹/₄ in.), glass, excavated from
Liao stupa dated to AD1044

4.11 Vase, dark brownish with
engraved design, h 26.4 cm (10³/₈ in.),
glass, excavated from a stupa of
Liao period temple, 11th century

4. In 1976–7, a Liao tomb at Guyingzi in Chaoyang city, Liaoning province, yielded a handled plain cup and a dish with mold-impressed design. The tomb dates from AD 1020.[15]

5. In 1988, the North pagoda of the Liao period in Chaoyang city, Liaoning province, yielded a plain ewer (see Fig. 4.10). The pagoda goes back to AD 1044.[16]

6. In 1988, the White pagoda of the Dule temple in Jixian county, Tianjin city, yielded a dish-mouthed narrow-necked vase with cut linear design (see Fig. 4.11).[17] The pagoda dates from AD 1058.

The Islamic glass unearthed from Song and Liao sites are largely products of Iran, though a small number were made in Egypt and on the eastern Mediterranean coast. Such glassware from the Liao tombs and pagodas of North China must have been imported by land, while those from South China were introduced by sea.

The Islamic glass unearthed in China show two distinctive features. It is, first of all, in most cases intact and of exquisite quality, and secondly, it possesses chronological exactness since all the artifacts come from dated tombs or similar sites.

NOTES

1. *Wenwu* (*Cultural Relics*), (1988), no. 10, p. 24
2. *Idemitsu Museum of Art Bulletin* (*Biju tsukan kampo*), Idemitsu Museum of Art, (1997), p. 20, Pls 47, 49, 52, 53
3. *Kaogu Xuebao* (*Acta Archaeologica Sinica*), (1984), no. 4, p. 420, Pl. V, 4
4. *BMFEA* (*Bulletin of the Museum of Far Eastern Antiquities*), no. 10, (1938), p. 13, Pl. III, 1
5. *Kaogu* (*Archaeology*), (1994), no. 5, p. 419
6. *Wenwu* (*Cultural Relics*), (2000), no. 1, p. 95
7. *Wenwu* (*Cultural Relics*), (1991), no. 5, p. 4
8. *Idemitsu Museum of Art Bulletin*, note 2, Pls 48, 50
9. *Wenwu* (*Cultural Relics*), (1972), no. 1, p. 77, Fig. 9
10. *Wenwu* (*Cultural Relics*), (1973), no. 1, p. 52, and cover page 3, 2
11. *Kaogu Xuebao* (*Acta Archaeologica Sinica*), (1956), no. 3, p. 16
12. *Wenwu* (*Cultural Relics*), (1975), no. 12, p. 27
13. Lane, (1947), London, p. 12, Pl. 4E
14. *Wenwu* (*Cultural Relics*), (1987), no. 11, p. 18, Pl. VI, 1 and 2
15. *Kaoguxue Jikan* (*Papers on Chinese Archaeology*), (1983), no. 3, p. 185, Pl. XXXIII, 1 and 3
16. *Lioahai Wenwu Xuekan* (*Liaohai Cultural Relics Journal*), (1990), no. 2, p. 20, Pl. V, 5
17. *Kaogu Xuebao* (*Acta Archaeologica Sinica*), (1989), no. 1, p. 108, Pl. XXIV, 5

(Translated by Mo Runxian)

中国出土的伊斯兰玻璃

马文宽

（中国社会科学院考古研究所）

　　唐高宗永徽二年（公元651年）阿拉伯帝国与中国建立了外交关系，此后两国交往频繁，商贸发展极为迅猛。精美的伊斯兰玻璃运销到中国。司马光在《资治通鉴》中记载，唐代岭南节度使路嗣恭于775年在广州从"舶商"那里掠得玻璃盘（直径达9寸——1尺）送给宰相和皇帝。可见伊斯兰大玻璃盘在8世纪下半叶已运销中国，并被视为极珍贵的物品。《宋史·外国传》记载，大中祥符四年（1011年）大食向宋真宗进贡"碧白琉璃酒器"。这些记载均被近几十年的考古发掘所证实。

　　出土唐代的伊斯兰玻璃有四处：

　　1. 1987年陕西省扶风县法门寺地宫出土刻花玻璃盘4件、刻花描金盘2件（图版1）、釉彩玻璃盘1件（图版2）、印花直筒杯2件（图版3）、贴花盘口瓶1件[1]。塔基建筑年代为唐干符元年（公元874年）。因此这些玻璃器均应在9世纪中期以前，可早到8世纪后半叶。这些玻璃器上的纹饰多与美索不达米亚的相同，应产自该地区。有学者根据伊朗尼沙布尔也出有这样的玻璃盘，认为法门寺的玻璃盘应产自尼沙布尔。这是欠妥的。因尼沙布尔在9–10世纪仅是个政治、军事中心。它在此时虽以生产陶器闻名，但也没有生产出精妙的拉斯特彩陶器和锡釉青花陶器，更生产不出如此高质量的玻璃器。

　　2. 1969年河北定县静志寺塔基地宫出有蓝、白直桶杯各1件，细颈瓶2件（图版4），方形小瓶1件。塔基始建于北魏兴安2年（453年），经隋、唐、宋四次重修。根据塔内"重建静志寺真身舍利塔铭"和"唐定州静志寺重葬真身记"载，这几件伊斯兰玻璃应属于9世纪[2]。

　　3. 洛阳市关林118号唐墓出土1件短细颈扁腹瓶[3]。1928年加拿大神父怀履光（White, W. C.）从洛阳掠走一批文物，其中有1件与此瓶相似的短细颈扁腹瓶[4]。此两瓶应是盛香水的瓶子，年代为8–9世纪。

　　4. 1990–1991年在扬州发掘一处唐晚期建筑址，可能是胡商居住的"邸店"，出土二百余片玻璃碎片，均不能复原成形[5]。据科学测试报告，这些玻璃属伊斯兰玻璃[6]。

　　出土五代的伊斯兰玻璃有一处：

　　1981年福建省福州市郊区发掘一座闽王墓，出有伊斯兰玻璃碎片。该墓年代为932年[7]。

　　出土宋代伊斯兰玻璃有三处：

　　1. 前述定州静志寺塔基地宫还出有刻花细颈玻璃瓶1件和深蓝色玻璃瓶1件（图版5），应是10世纪的伊斯兰玻璃。因地宫封藏年代为977年，故此二瓶年代应为10世纪中叶或以前[8]。

　　2. 1971年安徽省无为县舍利塔基出土刻花细颈玻璃瓶1件（图版6），其形制与纹饰均与定州静志寺塔基地宫出土的相同[9]。此塔建于公元1036年。

　　3. 1966–1967年浙江省瑞安县慧光塔出土刻花盘口球腹细颈玻璃瓶1件（图版7）。此塔建于1043年[10]。

　　辽墓辽塔出土的伊斯兰玻璃有六处：

　　1. 1954年内蒙古赤峰市辽墓出有小口玻璃瓶残片。此墓年代为公元959年[11]。

2.1974年辽宁省法库县叶茂台早期辽墓出土一件绿色方形玻璃调料盘[12]。此盘与伦敦不列颠博物馆藏黄绿釉方形调料盘相似。此陶盘上有阿拉伯铭文"巴士拉的阿卜纳斯尔在埃及制造"[13]。因而该玻璃方盘应产自伊斯兰之地的伊拉克或埃及。

3.1986年内蒙古奈曼旗辽墓出土刻花盘口细颈瓶1件、素面把杯（图版8）2件、磨花把杯1件、磨雕纹盘（图版9）1件、高颈瓶2件。此墓年代为公元1018年[14]。

4.1976–1977年辽宁省朝阳市姑营子辽墓出土素面把杯1件、印纹盘1件。此墓年代为1020年[15]。

5.1988年辽宁省朝阳市辽代北塔出土素面执壶（图版10）1件，此塔年代为1044年[16]。

6.1988年天津市蓟县独乐寺白塔出土磨刻花盘口细颈瓶（图版11）1件[17]。此塔年代为1058年。

宋辽时期出土的伊斯兰玻璃多数产自伊朗，少量的产自埃及和地中海东岸。北方辽墓辽塔出土的伊斯兰玻璃应从陆路输入，而南方出土的则是从海路输入。

中国出土的伊斯兰玻璃有两个特点。第一是大多数为完整器而精美。第二是都有精确的埋葬年代。

1.《文物》，1988年10期，24页。
2.《地下宫殿の遗宝—中国河北省定州北宋塔基出土文物展》，Idemitsu Museum of Arts, 1997, p. 20, pl. 47, 49, 52, 53。
3.《考古学报》，1984年4期，420页，图版伍，4。
4. BMFEA, No. 10, 1938. p. 13, pl. III, 1.
5.《考古》，1994年5期，419页。
6.《文物》2000年1期，95页。
7.《文物》1991年5期，4页。
8. 同2，图版48，50。
9.《文物》，1972年1期，77页，图9。
10.《文物》，1973年1期，52页，封三，2。
11.《考古学报》，1956年3期，16页。
12.《文物》，1975年12期，27页。
13. Early Islamic Pottery, p. 12, pl. 4E, London, 1947.
14.《文物》，1987年11期，18页，图版六，1、2。
15.《考古学集刊》，1983年3期，185页，图版叁叁，1、3。
16.《辽海文物学刊》，1990年2期，20页，图版五，5。
17.《考古学报》，1989年1期，108页，图版贰肆，5。

5

Poem of the Glass Bowl

Bhaihajya Guru Vaidurya Prabhasa is the Buddha of Medicine, who heals all including that of ignorance. In Chinese, this long name has been translated as *Yao shi liuli guang rulai* 藥師琉璃光如來 – Buddha of Glass Light, Master of Medicine, – who attracted widespread devotion from the fifth century onwards. There are several *sûtra* related to him, including the *Yao wang liuli guang jing* 藥王琉璃光經 – *Sûtra* of the Healing King of Glass Light. This was translated from Sanskrit into Chinese by Xuan Zang, the famous seventh century Buddhist pilgrim who went to India, and deposited the Sanscrit texts which he brought back from there in the Pagoda of the Great Wild Goose Daytana in Xi'an. A Five Dynasties (907–60) painting in the collection of the British Museum, shows the Buddha holding a translucent glass alms bowl, which the artist has embellished with clusters of blue dots. The dots bring to mind the blue glass applications found on eastern Roman glass vessels.[1]

Archaeological finds suggest that Roman glass vessels were imported by sea, which agrees with evidence found in ancient writings. For instance, the annals of the Han (206 BC–AD 220) dynasty record that the emperor Wu sent people across the seas to buy glass, and the *Periplus of the Erythraean Sea*, written probably late in the first century AD, mentions Chinese products as well as the transportation of glass. In northern China, however, trade must have relied on the overland route – the Silk Road – which according to one authority, could also be called the 'Glass Road'. Fragments of Roman glass found in many places in Xianjian support this theory, and the Western Jin dynasty (265–316) poet Pan Ni 潘尼, in an ode to a glass bowl, wrote about the difficult eastward journey of foreign glass, enumerating the stages of dangerous passage through the scorching deserts and over the steep peaks of the Pamirs.[2]

Other accounts tell of gifts of glass sent from the Roman empire, and the introduction of its techniques by western glassmakers, which took place almost simultaneously, both at the court of the Northern Wei (386–535) and that of the Liu Song (420–79) in the south, towards the middle of the fifth century. Earlier references to learning from western glassmaking technology were recorded in Chinese literature for the Wei and Jin dynasties (first–third century). It is related that the family of Wang Wuzi 王武子(家) of the Western Jin had glass platters for their food, and drank from glass bell-shaped cups and bowls. The texts do not specify the source for these vessels, but given the status of the owner, we can suggest that they were probably imported.

The most widely worshiped *Bodhisattva* in China was Guanyin 觀音, the Chinese name for *Avalokitêshvara*, the Compassionate Savior. The goddess appeared in a number different manifestations. One of them was the 'Glass Guanyin' (*Liuli Guanyin*), whose image was identified by a glass vessel – usually a ewer – held in the hands and by the figure's stance on a large lotus petal. After she was seen in a wondrous vision on the island of Putuo off the coast of Zhejiang province, near Hangzhou, another aspect of her emerged, the Water and Moon Guanyin.[3] In the painting from the Nelson-Atkins Museum of Art (49–60), the goddess is shown seated at ease on a rock, circled with a full moon – the most distinctive feature of her new iconography – and a vase for holding purifying water (see Fig. 5.1). The moon and water, or the reflection of the moon in water, were familiar Buddhist metaphors for the transitory and unsubstantial things of the world. Mention should be made of the clear vase set in a pale blue bowl. Since the body of the vase is visible through the translucent bowl, it is reasonable to assume that both vessels are made of glass.

At this time, the demand for glass in the form of reliquaries, dishes for liturgical offerings, and bowls for collecting alms, instigated the local manufacture of these wares. Indeed, the oldest glass Buddhist alms bowls excavated in China seems to be a Chinese product of pale green translucent glass dating to the fifth century. It was unearthed from the cemetary of the Feng family clan in Jingxian. Another Chinese alms bowl in opaque blue glass, was made some time before the sealing of a temple deposit in 481 at Dingzhou in Hebei province. Also discovered were five small glass bottles, three in the typically Chinese double-gourd shape, and over two thousand glass beads. The bottles may represent some of China's first blown glass. Their date is close to that of the *Wei Shu* 魏書 (Official history of the Wei dynasty) which provides a well-known record of glassmaking.

According to this account, in the early sixth century some Bactrian visitors were engaged to carry out what was afterwards hailed as a sensational production of glass tiles for a huge assembly hall in Pingcheng (modern Datong) in Shaanxi province. They made so much glass that it ceased to be a rarity. This caused Chinese products to depreciate alarmingly in value, and the local glass industry crashed. As a consequence, when the Sui took power (581) and established their new capital at the site of modern Xi'an, they found that there was no one who knew how to make glass. An ingenious courtier devised production of a form of paste which equated as nearly as possible with glass.

The enthusiasm for foreign glass led once to a most uncomfortable audience with an emperor. It seems that the Islamic glass dishes Lu Sigong 路嗣恭 had acquired, (see Chapter 4), differed in size. The one he presented to Daizong

代宗 (*r*.762–79) measured nine Chinese inches (*cun* 寸) in diameter. Initially, the sovereign was delighted to have acquired such an extreme rarity, that was until it emerged that Lu had presented a slightly larger dish measuring ten inches (approx. 30 cm) to an influential minister. This fatal difference of size was construed as a grave breach of etiquette. What is more significant, however, is that these 'rarities' had been shipped with other foreign goods from the Persian Gulf to Guangzhou, and that they were highly esteemed by the elite.[4]

Zhao Rugua 趙汝适, a member of the Imperial family under the Song (960–1279), held the position of superintendent of customs. He used his contacts with Arab, Persian and Indian merchants to advantage, and collected a store of information on foreign countries, which he published in two volumes under the title of *Zhufanji* 諸蕃志. Zhao mentions the superior quality of the colored and opaque glassware made in the countries of Islam, which was 'cut into patterns' or 'engraved', and annealed, and that the glass was highly prized in China. He also reported that, despite strict regulations, merchants could easily bypass the official system for tariff duties.[5] Just as quickly as the items arrived and were inspected and weighed for dues, they flowed out again into the street markets and shops and were sold to anyone speaking the international language of commerce.

A small group of Islamic enameled glass vases present an interesting conundrum. Their shapes imitate those of Longquan celadon (*yuhuchun ping* 玉壺春瓶) vases, examples of which are known from the Sinan wreck (probably 1320s) in East Java, from the Ardebil shrine in the Chihil Sutun in Isfahan and from the Topkapi Saray in Istanbul. The Chinese originals of the glass vases of this type have dragon-handles with pendant rings, here atrophied to disks at the base of the handles, while all that remains of the dragons' heads is squiggles above the handles (see Fig. 5.3). One example is lavishly decorated with chinoiserie flowers and foliage on a ground of blue enamel. Other motifs include phoenix or dragons in roundels, even a Buddhist lion cavorting with balls and ribbons. These motifs play an important part in the decorative scheme.[6] Although the relationship between these wares has yet to be researched, one can see the connections between glass on the one hand, and porcelain on the other, and the mutual influences between them. This blurring of distinctions was perhaps both a normal and inevitable consequence of the lucrative inflow and outflow of luxury items through Chinese trading posts.

Over one hundred European travelers, traders, and missionaries visited China during the Yuan era. In 1338, an entourage of sixteen under the leadership of Genovese, Andalo da Savigone, a merchant inhabitant of Beijing, arrived in Avignon bearing letters for the pope. The first letter was from the Shundi 順帝 emperor (*r*.1341–68), the other from the Latin Christians in China. Both letters asked for the 'frequent sending of envoys'. Pope Benedict XII speedily acted upon the request, and selected Fra Giovanni di Marignolli to head a legation. The pontiff endowed the retinue with rich gifts, including a mandate to purchase, as requested,

5.1 *Water and Moon Guanyin*, hanging scroll, ink, slight color and gold on silk, 111.1 × 76.2 cm (43³/₄ × 30 in.), late 13th–early 14th century, The Nelson-Atkins Museum of Art, Kansas City, Missouri (Purchase: Nelson Trust) 49–60

5.2 Burial vase, sea-green with surface pitting and iridescence, h 8.9 cm (3⁵/₈ in.), glass, Six dynasties period (220–581), private coll.

5.3 Vase, enameled Mamluk glass, Gustav Schmoranz, *Old Oriental gilt and enamelled glass vessels*, London, 1899, Plate V

the finest horses for the emperor, and a splendid crystal vase and glassware from Venice.[7] Marignolli arrived in Beijing in 1342. He traveled extensively during his four-year visit, and never stopped marveling at the life being led in China's cities by his fellow Europeans.

It is a truism known to every historian that China goes through cycles when it is 'open' or 'closed' to the West. During the turbulent change from the Yuan (1271–1368) to the Ming dynasty (1368–1644), one fact of life under the Mongol rulers became increasingly untenable: the presence of foreign merchants and their communities. Assimilation was halted and China turned back upon itself.

The most substantial record of glassmaking for the Ming period is found in a work by Sun Tingquan 孫廷銓, the *Yanshan zaji* 顔山雜記 (*Mt. Yan Miscellaney*). Sun was born into a family of officials who for several generations had supervised the making of glass at Zibo in Shandong. In the third year of the Hongwu 洪武 reign (1370), a Sun Kerang 孫克讓 was recruited to serve as a glass artisan at the Imperial Household Workshops in Beijing. Thereafter, members of the Sun family worked on rotation between Zibo and the capital. They went on to become supervisors and, as such, were ultimately responsible for the production of glass in both places.[8]

Zibo was located on the Shalu river, a place which encompassed the old town area of Yanshen (Boshan). The area was rich in natural resources and, with its links to the Grand Canal, was well suited to supply other parts of China with glassware. It is not clear when glassmaking started at Zibo, but records of the Sun family, recovered artifacts, and the remains of furnaces suggest the late Yuan dynasty and early Ming period.[9] According to *Qingzhou fuzhi* 青州府志 (*Records of Qingzhou Prefecture*), Yanshen glass was made entirely from local materials: feldspar, fluorspar, quartz, niter, brass, iron, cinnabar, and lead.[10] Excavation of the site at Zibo exposed the foundations of twenty furnace pits arranged in a line, where glass of different colors was worked into ornaments. A larger central furnace produced glass from raw materials to be worked up in the smaller ones. Glass beads, hair clasps, and ornaments, together with the remains of clay pots and waste glass were gathered as samples for testing. It was determined that the melting furnaces had been fueled by coke, which is also noted in ancient Chinese literature. The glass samples showed that forming techniques, such as tube-drawing, molding, and various types of off-hand processing, were used in the ancient glassworks.[11]

Zhao had pointed out that the main ingredients used in Song glass included lead, saltpeter (niter) lime (plaster stone), and gypsum, which revealed for the first time that the glass of southern China included soda-lime compositions.[12] This was found to be similar to the composition for the glasses described in Sun's text, and in accordance with the results of an investigative report from the 1930s.[13] Since the craftsmen of this time lacked sophisticated tools and instruments, they gauged the temperature of the molten glass by examining the color of the flames. The

44

guide for this seems to have been that the charcoal flames were at first 'black' and leaping. As the molten substance became purified, the flames assumed a red tone, then blue, and eventually white. 'Feldspar', he wrote was used for the body, 'fluorite for the softening [fluxing], and quartz for luster.'[14]

It has to be admitted that Sun's batch recipes do not always make very good glassmaking sense, but they do show that glass was made in ten shades of crystal, white, crimson, blue, golden-yellow, transparent blue, ivory-white, true black, green and gosling-yellow. For instance, the glass artifacts recovered from the second stratum of the Zibo excavations comprised rings, hairpins made of opaque turquoise or white glass (see Fig. 5.5), and beads, some of transparent lime-green glass, some black and yellow. Sun describes the making of *chansi* 纏絲 glass (thread-spun glassware) by spinning threads of different colored glass evenly around the workpiece. Most of the objects mentioned are ornaments but hollow-blown vessels are discussed, such as bulbs, fish-shaped vases, and gourds. Cast objects included blue glass lead curtains, pendants and chess pieces. These findings confirm the existence of this ancient glassworks, and attest to its considerable scale of production.

Related wares that may have come from Zibo have been noted in the tombs of the Yuan and very early Ming periods: a pale blue cup molded in the form of a lotus, a white *gui* 圭 (sceptre) in imitation of jade; and colorless beads.[15] The tomb of Zhu Tan 朱檀 (*d.*1389) yielded black and white glass gaming pieces for a *weiqi* (圍棋). Continuity of manufacture can be substantiated from a number of late Ming sources, such as Song Yingxing 宋應星. In his 1637 work *Tiangong kaiwu*

5.4 Cup, with elongated lotus panels and animal head handles, brownish white, h 6 cm (2³/₈ in.), late 17th−18th century, glass coll. William Lillyman

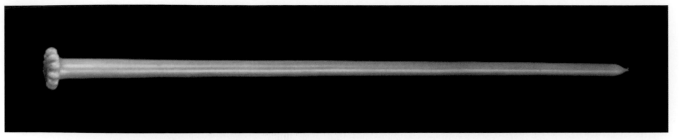

5.5 Hairpin with molded floral design, opaque turquoise, l 19.7 cm (7³/₄ in.), Ming dynasty (1368–1644), glass, private coll.

天工開物 (*Matter laid open by heaven's operation*), Song described the making of beads and lanterns and located the glassmaking industry in Shandong. The type of ware under production may be illustrated by *Chrysanthemums*, a hanging scroll in the collection of the British Museum, bearing the signature of Chen Hongshou 陳洪綬 and a 1635 date (see Fig. 5.6). It shows a colorless, transparent bottle of ovoid form with a slightly concave base and judging by the size of the flowers, the stems of which are visible through the glass, it could have stood some 300 mm high. Further evidence of the late Ming manufacture of glass has been supplied by the recovery of cargo from a Chinese wreck of about 1600 off the Philippines. It yielded wound beads in clear red and opaque white, and yellow and turquoise glass.[16]

Song Yingxing also related in his work that the droughts during the thirteenth and fourteenth years of the reign of Chongzhen 崇禎 (*r*.1628–43), decimated the population of the Yanshen area which disrupted production for a generation. In the closing years of the Ming dynasty, the Manchu troops swept down from the north destabilizing the country, and not until early in the reign of Kangxi 康熙 (*r*.1662–1722) did glass manufacture begin to flourish again at Yanshenzhen.

NOTES
1. Whitefield (1982–3), vol. 2 Fig. 20, also Moore (1998), p. 82
2. An Jiayao, in Brill and Martin (1991), pp. 5–19
3. Yu Chunfang (1994), pp. 151–78
4. Moore (1998), pp. 80–1
5. Zhao Rugua (1911), pp. 17, 228
6. Rogers (1998), pp. 72–3
7. Arnold (1999), p. 95. ('... en decident d'apporter à l'empereur des verreries et des joyaux de cristal; il ne pouvait s'en procurer de plus beaux qu' à Venise. Cette decision n'est pas originale')
8. Zhang Weiyong (2000), p. 76
9. Yi Jialiang and Tu Shujin (1991), p. 99
10. Yang Boda (1991), p. 138
11. Yi Jialing and Tu Shujin (1991), pp. 99–100
12. Yang Boda (1991), p. 137
13. Yang Boda (1991), p. 138
14. Yang Boda (1984), p. 9
15. See Shandong Provincial Museum, 'Fajue Ming Zhu Tan mu jishi', *Wenwu*, 1972, no. 5, pp. 25–36
16. Hardie (1990), pp. 10–11

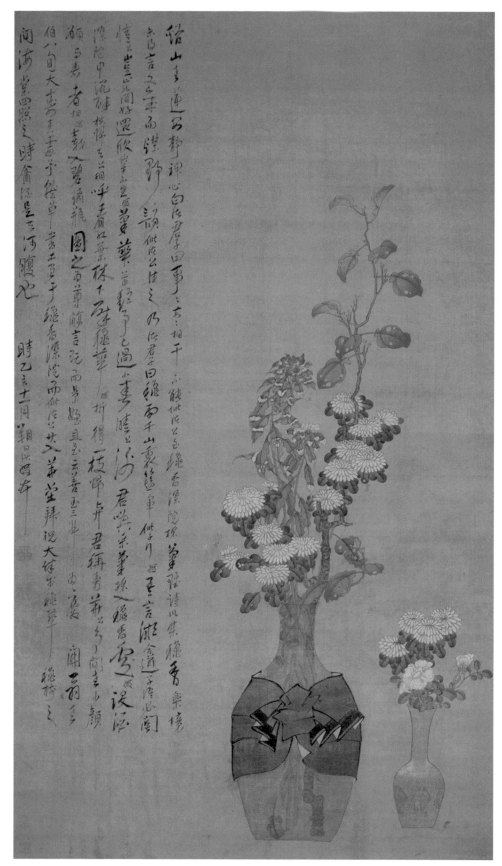

5.6 Chen Hongshu, *Chrysanthemums*, ink and colors on paper, inscription, date of 1635, 175 × 98 cm (68³/₄ × 38¹/₂ in.), Trustees of the British Museum, Dept. of Oriental Antiquities

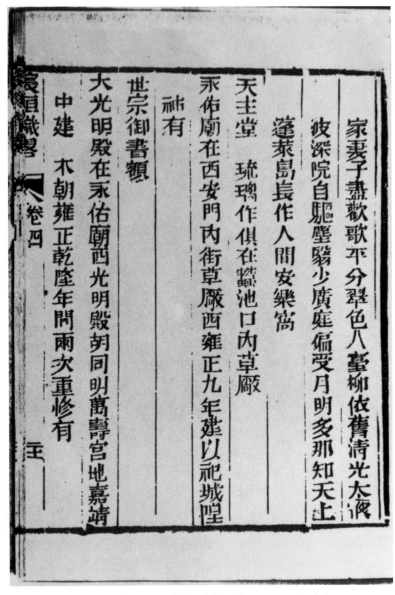

家麗子盡歡歌平分絳色八臺柳依舊清光太液

波深院自驅蟾窺少廣庭偏受月明多那知天上

蓬萊島長作人間安樂窩

天主堂　琉璃作俱在蠶池口內草廠

永佑廟在西安門內街草廠西雍正九年建以祀城隍

神有

世宗御書額

大光明殿在永佑廟西光明殿胡同明萬壽宮地嘉靖

中建　本朝雍正乾隆年間兩次重修有

宸垣識略　卷四

6.1 Wu Changyuan, *Chenyuan shihlueh* (1788), extract pertaining to location of the glassworks

6

'Complete Plan of the Glass Workshop'

It has been said that art forms reflect changing political and economic status. In 1644, the Qing replaced the Ming emperors, and pursued a course of greater engagement with the world. Under their patronage, Chinese glassmaking experienced a of unprecedented development. Traditional Chinese glass technology was allied, through missionaries, to European innovations. Thus, a new aesthetic was created by, and from, the changed political reality. And, as related to the subject at hand, Yang Boda described the resulting fusion as the 'flowering of Chinese glass'.[1]

According to the *Xichao ding'an* 熙朝定案 (*Episodes of a prosperous age*), in the second month, twenty-eighth year of Kangxi (1689), the emperor, having reached Hangzhou during his southern tour, received from the Jesuit missionary, Prospero Intorcetta (Yin Duoze 殷鐸澤), the gift of a polychrome glass sphere. Another missionary is recorded as having presented the emperor with a small telescope, a hand mirror, and two glass vases.[2] These gifts of European glass were greatly appreciated by Kangxi, and may have prompted him to seek missionary assistance in setting up an Imperial glass workshop.

The most important official documents complied by the Qing court are the *Da Qing huidian* 大清會典 (*A Collection of the Rules and Regulations of the Great Qing*), and the *Da Qing huidian shili* 大清會典事例 (*Examples and Incidents Relating to the Rules and Regulations of the Great Qing*). Therefore, in order to obtain a complete picture of the regulations governing the glass workshop, both parts need to be consulted. The relevant passage in the latter records the establishment of a glass workshop in the thirty-fifth year of Kangxi (1696), and that it was under the jurisdiction of the Zaobanchu 造辦處 (Imperial Household Department).[3] This workshop is mentioned also in two eighteenth century texts, Zhu Yizun's (朱彝尊) well-known history of Beijing and its environs, the *Rixia Jiuwen Kao* 日下舊聞考,[4] and a work by Wu Changyuan 吳長元 (*Chenyuan shihlueh* 宸垣識略),[5] with the latter in the section devoted to describing the Imperial city (see Fig. 6.1). Both texts state that glass is made in a workshop next to the Catholic Church – the French Jesuits' one – on *Canchikou* 蠶池口, the name of the street along the east side of the complex. This is not only consistent with the markings found on Chinese maps for this period, but confirms the accuracy of a diagram the missionaries made of the site.[6]

Kangxi had given the French fathers a house within the enclosure of the *huang cheng* 皇城 (yellow walls) of the Imperial city, in 1693, as a signal favor for having cured him of malaria, and the following year the emperor presented them with an adjacent plot of ground for the building of their church. Jean de Fontaney, S. J. (Hong Ruohan 洪若翰) wrote several letters about the establishment of the workshop, the most detailed being the one dated 31 October 1696. It reads: 'The Emperor is making a beautiful glassworks next to our house on a large piece of land'.[7] Continuing, Fontaney points to Kilian Stumpf, S. J. (Ji Lian 紀理安) as the reason for this; he requests a glassworker to make glass and crystal, and emphasizes that this is being done not for commercial purposes, but to please the emperor. Stumpf had come to China with many scientific skills among which was glass-making, and Kangxi based his decision to summon him to Beijing, upon the reports officials in Guangzhou had submitted attesting to his expertise in this area.

Recorded in the traditional manner, the Chinese plan (see Fig. 6.2) of the glassworks[8] bears an inscription on the lower portion (see Fig. 6.3). It reads:

Complete Plan of the Glass Workshop

Twelve rooms (*jian* 間)

Five surrounding buildings

Each inch on the plan equals: one foot (*chi* 尺) on the ground

On the northern boundary, Official Street (*Guanjie* 官街), altogether from east to west 10 *zhang* 丈, 8 *chi*

On the southern boundary, the Roman Catholic church (*Tianzhutang* 天主堂), from west to east 12 *zhang*, 5 *chi*

On the eastern boundary, the Roman Catholic church (*Tianzhutang*), from south to north 11 *zhang*, 6 *chi*

On the western boundary, neighboring resident families, from north to south 26 *zhang*.

Bearing in mind that 'north' is at the bottom of the Chinese plan, the building on the far right is labeled 'West out-building, three *jian* (spans)', and that the corresponding building, diagonally opposite, on the upper left, is labeled 'East out-building, three *jian*'. The 'Main Gate' is bottom center, and just above this is the largest building or group of buildings. In the inscription, the part on the right is labeled 'west open veranda, one jian'. It may be observed that while the characters *baoxia* 抱廈 are often translated as 'surrounding building', a *baoxia* can be also an open porch attached to a building. This complex has such open porches also at the top and bottom, and the central part is labeled 'kiln/furnace room, three *jian*' (see Fig. 6.4). An indication as to their overall appearance might be gained from an illustration in Johann Künckel's *Ars vitraria experimentalis* (see Fig. 6.5), published in 1679. Its most notable feature is the open pavilion-like construction, with the sides open for ventilation – an important consideration for the

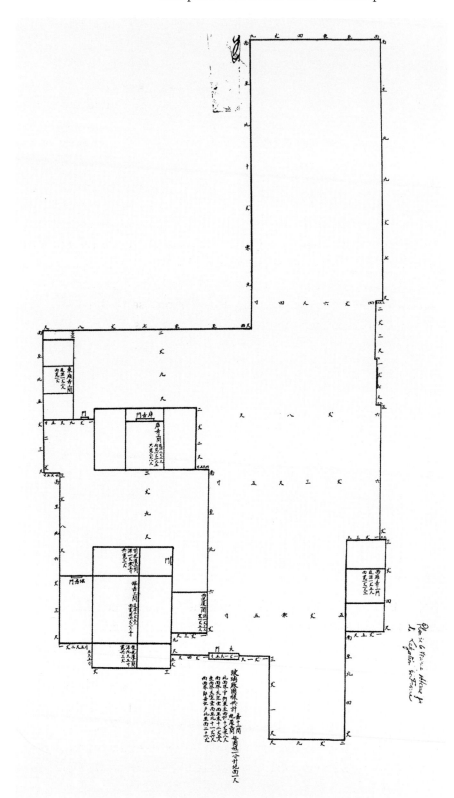

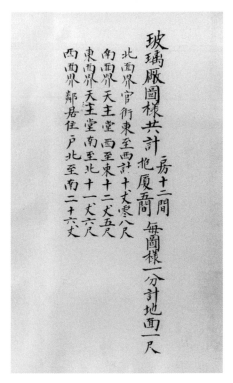

6.3 Detail, 6.2, with bottom center inscription

6.2 Chinese plan of missionary glass workshop, 90.1 × 44.5 cm (35³/₈ × 17¹/₂ in.), probably 18th century, Archives Congrégation de la Mission Lazaristes, Maison-Mère, Paris

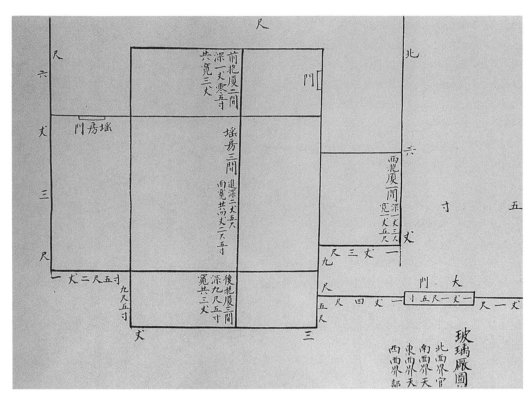

6.4 Detail, 6.2, with main gate and building with kiln

6.5 A glass workshop with ovens, glassblowers and attendants. *Ars vitraria experimentalis*, Johann Künckel, 1679, p. 334

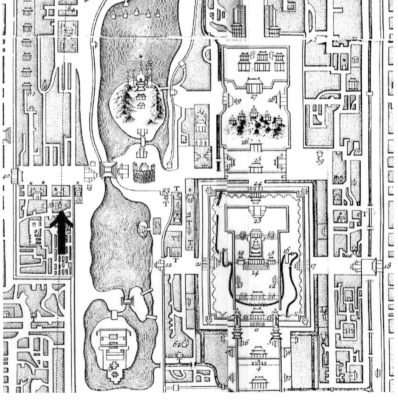

6.6 Detail of map made by the missionaries, the glass workshop is located to the left of the Forbidden City, *Description de la Ville de Péking*, D. Delisle, 1765

furnaces. The remaining building, left/center on the plan, is labeled 'storehouse, three *jian*'.[9]

Anxious to staff the workshop, the French Jesuits arranged for two glass workers, identified only as Vilette and d'Andigné, to be sent to Beijing in 1699. At least one of them (probably d'Andigné), was presented to the Kangxi emperor, and accepted for employment at the Imperial workshop.[10] While it would be interesting to know exactly what these two glass craftsmen did during their stay in the capital, no additional information has yet surfaced concerning them. More importantly, the workshop was staffed with talented Chinese artisans. These 'disciples' of Stumpf's 'glassmaking art'[11] would have included some of the craftsmen summoned from glassmaking centers in Yanshen and Guangzhou to serve at the Imperial glassworks. They learned from Stumpf the practice of molding the material into desired shapes, producing pleasing colors, and using the wheel to engrave and polish.[12]

Lodovico Antonio Appiani, C. M. (Bi Tianxiang 畢天祥) mentioned (1708) being in a room full of young artisans, who were carving floral patterns on glassware (*che con un hordegno a' ruota scolpiscono fiori sopra il vetro*).[13] Also, Appiani's description matches closely an entry in the *Da Qing huidian* on the 'glasshouse' which says that in addition to 'furnace rooms for the making and blowing of glassware . . . there are grinding rooms for carrying out the fine work on the material'.[14]

Additional documentation suggests that this workshop was already producing high-quality wares by the first years of the eighteenth century. For instance, Wang Shizhen's (王士禎) *Xiangzu biji* 香祖筆記 (1702), makes reference to glass snuff bottles produced by the Imperial workshop in a great variety of shapes and colors. The white is described as being like crystal, while the red is compared to that of fire. Other colors given are purple, yellow, black, and green.[15] Another official, Gao Shiqi 高士奇, succeeded in pleasing Kangxi by not only comparing the glassware from the Imperial workshop favorably to European examples, but by observing that 'Now China can produce [glass] far surpassing that of the West.'[16]

Unfortunately, the nature and appearance of the twenty pieces of glass the emperor subsequently bestowed upon him (1703), was not recorded. In the forty-fourth year of Kangxi (1705), the emperor traveled to Suzhou, south of the Yangtze river, and gave the official Song Luo 宋犖 gifts that had been made by his glass artisans. The group included a transparent fish-bowl, a sparkling blue glass vase, a small yellow glass dish, and a blue glass brush holder with floral design, and totaled seventeen pieces.[17]

On 25 February 1706, Kangxi presented the papal legate, Maillard de Tournon (Duo Luo 多羅), with an enameled glass snuff bottle (*una tabaccherina di vetro smaltata*).[18] As corroboration of this incident, the description tallies with the inventory of de Tournon's personal effects, made in 1712.[19] The reference is significant, to the world of Chinese art, in that it antedates by ten years the

6.7 Censer, on raised feet with two handles, marbled opaque blue, l 10.2 cm (4 in.), glass, attributed to 18th century, private coll.

6.8 Snuff bottle, opaque sapphire blue incised with a *fenghuang* holding a peony spray, h 5.9 cm (2¼ in.), glass, two character *Kangxi* mark (1662–1722) on base, coll. M. M. Young

previously accepted date for Kangxi enameled glassware, that is, the four pieces recorded in the *Gongzhong dang kangxichao zouzhe* 宮中檔康熙朝奏摺 for 1716, a red glass snuff bottle with polychrome decoration, an octagonal ink stone box, a desk top water pot, and a round incense container.[20]

Palace records indicate that two Guangzhou artisans, Cheng Xianggui 程向貴 and Zhou Jun 周俊 worked in the glassworks for at least seven years (1709–15). Cheng is said to have made a set of twelve cups with floral pattern, having a color described as 'the blue of the sky after rain' (*yuguo tianqing* 雨過天晴), which were offered to the court in the forty-eighth year of Kangxi (1709). Zhou, in the fifty-fourth year (1715), fired a plain set of glass cups also in 'the blue of the sky after rain'.[21] In that same year Matteo Ripa (Ma Guoxian 馬國賢) observed that the workshop had expanded to include many furnaces for glassmaking, all that was needed for a great number of craftsmen, and everything else that was needed for a strong glassworks, which apparently required Stumpf's constant attention.[22] Despite the progress of the glassworks, it is evident that Kangxi was not entirely satisfied with the efforts of his enamel artisans, since he repeatedly asked the missionaries presented to him if they possessed this skill.

Some help was provided when the governor of Guangdong, sent (1716) two craftsmen with enameling skills from his region, along with 'some Western enamel

6.9 Box, painted enamel on white with floral decoration, base with *Kangxi yuzhi mark*, d 5 cm (2 in.), glass, early 18th century, Haggs Gemeentemuseum, The Hague, O.G. 34. 1931, Photograph by Jan Zweerts

6.10 Detail of 6.9 with *Kangxi yuzhi* mark

material, ... so that when they arrive Your Majesty may personally assess their abilities'.[23] However, the techniques of making painted enamel ware were still to be perfected, and Kangxi had to wait until 1719, for a trained enameler, in the person of the French Jesuit Jean-Baptiste Gravereau (Ni Tianjue 倪天爵).[24] The following year, Joseph de Moriac de Mailla, S. J. (Feng Bingcheng 馮秉正), sent a letter to Paris in which he described Gravereau's arrival at court, the work being done in enamel, and a reminder for the list of colors 'needed for the enamel; which will be used for the painting', and a plea for them to be sent as soon as possible.[25]

The National Palace Museum, Taipei, has in its collection what may be considered a reliable example of Kangxi enameled glassware, even though the piece bears no reign mark. This small vase is decorated with a design of peony blossoms in tones of burnt sienna, pink and apple green, on a background of indigo blue.[26] A white glass box in the Haggs Gemeentemuseum is painted in brilliant *famille rose* enamels on a yellow ground. Its flowers are in shades of red and blue, with the branches and leaves outlined in black and painted in green and brown. The base bears a well-written *Kangxi yuzhi* mark in light blue (see Fig. 6.9).

In 1721, Carlo Ambrogio Mezzabarba (Jia Luo 嘉樂), envoy of Pope Clement XI arrived in Beijing. To Kangxi's great regret, Gravereau was in poor health and wished to return to France. Thus when the papal envoy presented Niccolo Tomacelli at court, the emperor promptly set him to painting in enamel. As a result Tomacelli became a virtuoso in that medium.[27] The pope's gifts included pieces of Venetian glassware. They were offered to Kangxi on the morning of 2 January 1721. After expressing his pleasure and commenting upon their rarity, Ripa recorded the emperor's acceptance of the *cristalli di Venezia*.[28]

Kilian Stumpf died in July of 1720, some five months before Mezzabarba's arrival in Beijing, and in relating details of his life to the legate, Stumpf was described as having been the first to introduce and teach the art of making glass to the court of Beijing.[29] A final word on the glass workshop in this period may be found in Georg Johann Unverzagt's account of the Russian embassy. It says, 'After twenty days we left the French Jesuit Fathers to themselves and their church, . . . We came to their glass manufactory, so newly found in China, known also for the blowing of pretty glass. When we had all seen this we made our way home.'[30]

NOTES

1. Yang Boda (1991), p. 131
2. Chang (1987), p. 87
3. Lam (2000), pp. 37–9
4. Zu Yizun (1782), *juan* 14, 8b, also, Curtis (1999), pp. 147–8
5. Wu Changyuan (1778), *juan* 4, 21a, also, Curtis (1998), p. 101
6. A diagram, of the French Jesuits' complex is illustrated in Favier's *Péking*, p. 188
7. ARSI Jap/Sin 166, 136f, 31 October 1696
8. Guilbaud (1998), for further details see Curtis (2001)
9. Translation from the Chinese by John Finlay
10. Pelliot (1929), pp. 252–67
11. ARSI Jap/Sin 132, f263v, 15 October 1700

12. ARSI, Elogium 03f, uncatalogued, 1721, Ignatius Kögler
13. APF: *Scritture Originali della Congregazione Particolare dell' Indie e Cina*, vol. 11, f462v
14. Lam (2000), p. 39
15. Wang Shizhen (1705), *Xiangzu biji zixu*, 1705, juan 9, 7b
16. Gao Shiqi (1912–1913), vol. 2, p. 4b
17. Chang Lin-sheng (1991b), p. 45, #36
18. APF: *Scritture riferite nei Congressi*, vol. 9, 267v, 28 or 29 February 1706
19. APF: *Scritture riferite nei Congressi*, vol. 12, 344f, 27 April 1713
20. *Gongzhong dang Kangxi chao zou zhe* (1976), vol. 6, pp. 602–603
21. Archives, no. 3294, Yang Boda (1983), p. 16, #40
22. APF: *Scritture riferite nei Congressi*, vol. 14, 201v, May 1715
23. Chang Lin-sheng (1991a), p. 102
24. Chinese texts bearing Kangxi's corrections in vermilion and preserved in the Palace Museum record Gravereau's name as Ni Tianjue (see Rosso, pp. 338, 373–4). This differs from the name cited by Yang Boda (1987), p. 54
25. ARSI Jap/Sin 199 I, f251v, 16 October 1720
26. Chang Lin-sheng (1991a), p. 96, Figs. 3, 3a
27. Soulié de Morant (1916), p. 181
28. Archivio Generale OFM, MH8/1, 1721, p. 23
29. Biblioteca Nazionale Centrale di Firenze, Palatini 1115, XXVI, no. 20, [*Relazione sullo*], 452v.
30. Unverzagt, p. 94

7.1 Bowl, colorless, wheel engraved with a band of abstract scrolls, d 24.2 (9⁵/₈ in.), glass, late 17th–early 18th century, The Rohss Museum of Applied Art and Design, Sweden, No. 552–30

7

The *Rainha dos Anjos*:
Her Precious Cargo

Carlo Ambrogio Mezzabarba, the aforementioned papal legate, was amiably received by Kangxi, who entrusted him with many gifts for the pope.[1] On the eighteenth day [14 February 1721]:

> The August Emperor asked Jia Luo [Mezzabarba] thus: 'Can you take with you the things
> I wish to bestow on the King of Portugal?' Jia Luo answered that he could take them.
> Then the August Emperor commissioned Hon. Zhao (Chang) 趙昌 and Li (Guoping)
> 李國屛 to bestow . . . on the King of Portugal three pair of lanterns, plus two cases of
> porcelain ware, two cases of enamel ware, two cases of Japanese lacquer ware, and two
> cases of glassware. The August Emperor said: '. . . let Hon. Li look for, and make
> cases in which to ship these things.'[2]

Sometime prior to the legate's arrival at court, the emperor had mentioned that he was considering sending a Jesuit to Lisbon to thank the Portugese king for the gifts he had sent to Beijing. Kangxi wanted to reciprocate and decided that Mezzabarba's return voyage would be a fine opportunity to do so. He also realized that for reasons of protocol, he could not ask Mezzabarba to present the gifts since this would make the papal legate an envoy of the Chinese government. Antonio de Magalhães, S. J. (Zhang Anduo 張安多) was proposed as a suitable Imperial envoy to accompany Mezzabarba. Thus, after hearing Mezzabarba's affirmative reply, Kangxi gave Magalhães a box with thirteen pearls in it for the king and told him: 'You will say to the king of Portugal that I, the Emperor, with my own hands deliver this box to you in order that you may present [it] to him in his own hand on my behalf.'[3] In reference to his credentials, Magalhães wrote that he had been appointed a 'mandarin of the third order' (*Mandarini 3° ordinis insignitus*).[4] This meant that Magalhães was entitled to wear a square with a peacock on it, to indicate his official rank.

After a farewell audience, Mezzabarba and Magalhães traveled to Guangzhou and obtained passage on the *Rainha dos Anjos*. It set sail from Macau on 9 December 1721, for Brazil. The vessel entered the port of Rio de Janeiro 15 May 1722, and anchored in Guanabara Bay. Magalhães wanted the king's presents to be taken ashore and placed under the governor's jurisdiction. Mezzabarba, who did not regard Magalhães as a fully accredited envoy, insisted that they remain on board. So, it was with considerable dismay that the legate observed Magalhães going about Rio in a public display of authority, attired in a mandarin's robe, and attended by his Chinese servant. Regrettably, on 17 June 1722, the *Rainha dos Anjos* caught fire and sank along with its precious cargo. The governor ordered an immediate search for remains, but little was found, and except for an occasional mention in specialized historical works, the *Rainha dos Anjos* with her valuable cargo was largely forgotten.

This situation was dramatically altered with George Loehr's 1963 publication of a list of the gifts Kangxi had sent to the pope. Given that scholars had long debated the existence of Kangxi glass, the importance of this firm documentation for '136 vases made of Peiking glass', cannot be overstated, and it became a standard reference point for studies of early Qing glassware.[5] However, an encounter in Brazil, produced another document with important consequences for the study of Chinese glass.

It was a report[6] by Jean-François Foucquet, S. J. (Fu Shengze 傅聖澤), with a detailed list for the king of Portugal's gifts.[7] Foucquet left China shortly after Mezzabarba's departure and when his vessel, the *Prince de Conti*, missed the island of St Helena off the West African coast, it headed for Brazil, and reached the Bay of All Saints, Salvador on 9 May. Since the Portuguese suspected that the *Prince de Conti* was one of the notorious pirate ships then infecting the area, the governor of the Bay of All Saints, D. Vasco Fernandez César de Meneses, led a two-week inspection of the vessel. During this time, Meneses asked Foucquet to write a report about his work in China, and about the ship's voyage from Guangzhou. Foucquet appended his list of the gifts to this report.[8] Comprised of some thirty-nine entries, the catalogue includes lanterns, artificial flowers, books, papers, enamel ware, porcelain, tea, ginseng, glass, and pearls. For the glassware we find:

> Two plates of red glass.
> Eight small glass cups with flower [pattern] the color of blue sky after rain
> [*yuguo tianqing* 雨過天晴]. One chest.
> Ten small sky-blue [*tianlan* 天藍] plates.
> Ten medium [size] plates the color of celestial red [*de couleur rouge celeste*]. There are
> also five cups [which are] white inside and gilt on the outside.
> Two pots the color of blue sky after rain, adorned with flower [pattern] and decorated
> with figures, in the Chinese style. Dragons, etc.
> Two plates the color of blue sky after rain.
> Two plates of white glass ornamented with flowers.
> Two cups of white glass with lids [and] ornamented with designs of flowers.

The terms 'flowers' and 'flower pattern' are difficult to understand, and among the suggestions put forth is that it might refer to the type of floral pattern made by

7.2 Screen, colorless panel with diamond-point engraving, set in a hardwood stand, h 17.6 cm (7 in.), glass, 18th century, Christie's, London, 16 November 1998, #287

the 'grinding technique'. Appiani's eye-witness observation that the artisans were 'carving floral patterns' on the glass, and his reference to *un hordegno a ruota scolpiscono* suggests the use of a rotary wheel. Wheel-engraving has been defined as a process of decorating glass by means of a rotating wheel which grinds a pattern or inscription into the glass surface. One type of design consists of abstract scrolls or stylized dragons, sometimes surrounding a *shou* 壽 character, or as in the Rohsska Museum's bowl, a lotus blossom (see Fig. 7.1). The design was filled in with ink or some pigment, and is contained within a doubled line, a noteworthy feature which links it to some covered bowls with Yongzheng marks.

Diamond-point engraving was much in vogue in Europe during the seventeenth and eighteenth centuries, and it appears on Chinese vessels only after the establishment of the Imperial workshop (see Fig. 7.2). With this observation in mind, the Bristol Museum has in its collection a pair of cups which fit the description on Foucquet's list closely. The graceful hexagonal cups are fashioned of pale powder blue glass on the inside and bright cobalt blue outside, with diamond-point engraved decoration of flowers and scrolls, the grooves filled in with gilt.[9]

61

It is apparent from Foucquet's list that the Imperial glass workshop continued to make glass the color of 'blue sky after the rain', after the glassmakers, Cheng and Zhou, returned to Guangzhou in 1715, and in addition to cups, used this shade to fashion pots, plates, and perhaps vases. This description was probably derived from that of the mysterious Chai 柴 stoneware made during the reign of the emperor Shizong 世宗 (r.953–59), who commanded that the pieces fired should be the color of 'the blue of the sky after rain as seen in the rifts of clouds.'[10] The *Jingdezhen taolu* 景德鎮陶錄 records the production of a 'blue sky after rain' porcelain glaze by official and private workshops which specialized in large pieces. This light 'sky blue' glaze, sometimes referred to as *clair de lune*, was made throughout the Qing dynasty, and a remarkably similar tone may be found in glassware.[11]

Regrettably, the collection of the Palace Museum, Beijing contains only one example of glass from the reign of Kangxi. It is an hexagonally shaped transparent glass brush washer (*cheng* 丞) bearing the rare *Kangxi yuzhi* (made by the Imperial order of Kangxi) base mark. The *cheng*'s faceted body complete with cover, being alien to Chinese designs, owes in that respect, its origin to the European glass bottles made at the time. Attempts to identify items of glassware from this period have been hampered by a lack of other documentary pieces, and many attributions have been made on the basis of the glassware's crizzled metal. This opinion was first expressed more than a half century ago by W. B. Honey, who suggested also that this degradation might be associated with western craftsmen at the Imperial glassworks.[12]

7.3 Snuff bottle, colorless, crizzled, h 7 cm (2⁵/₈ in.), glass, late 19th–early 20th century, private coll.

Briefly stated, crizzling, is one variant of what has often been called 'sick glass' – a persistent, not very precise term referring to various forms of glass deterioration. These can range from a slightly cloudy or dulled appearance to a network of fine cracks (see Fig. 7.3). The 'disease' which leads to the deterioration of the glass, is caused by a faulty balance of the ingredients in the batch – specifically, an excess of alkali. This condition occurred in many pieces of European, east Asiatic, and American glass manufactured between the seventeenth and nineteenth centuries, and examples exist in public and private collections throughout the world. In 1975 the Corning Glass Works conducted a chemical analyses of some crizzled glass. Ten examples were chosen; they ranged from specimens of Venetian colorless glass from *c.*1709, to a Silesian vessel 1710–30, and a piece of American glass made in 1971. Results of these tests suggest that crizzling cannot be confined to a particular period or workshop, nor can this condition be used to confer provenance.[13]

Returning to Foucquet's list, we find a corroborating one in the Biblioteca Nacional de Lisboa.[14] This list, of unknown authorship, exhibits minor differences with Foucquet's more detailed descriptions. For instance, it gives '*vasa 42 ex vitro Pekinensi*', in comparison to Foucquet's mention of forty-three glass vessels. Also not mentioned are pieces of purple, yellow, black, and green glass color, nor is there any reference to the aventurine glass which was so highly prized.

Aventurine glass was a specialty of Venetian artisans, who were said to have discovered the art of making this glass (1640s) by accidently (*all' avventura*) dropping some copper filings into molten glass. Apropos of this, a letter in the French Jesuit archives reveals the efforts by the Kangxi's first son, Yinti 胤禔, who 'had a very inquiring nature and made big expenditures to make some lovely pieces in glass at his residence and offered them to the Emperor; his wish was to find a way to make pieces as beautiful as our Aventurine.'[15] Another indication of the demand for it in China may be found in the contents of an extremely rare presentation list from the Kangxi reign. All of the items on the list are imported goods presented to the emperor in 1722.[16] The entry translated as 'golden brown glass sphere, two pieces', is written with the characters for 'Gold star (*jinxing* 金星) glass', which is how the Chinese described aventurine. The term is not necessarily confined to brownish glass, and aventurine embellishments may include gold drops, gold flecks, and splashes of colored enamels. This explanation places into perspective several well-known vases of deep, transparent blue, mixed with bits of metallic-flecked glass (see Fig. 7.4). Vases made from this type of glass are thought to have been used for display purposes on side tables, and have been compared to porcelain objects sprinkled with gold.

Among other Chinese vessels which exhibit Venetian glassmaking techniques is a cup from the Dagan collection (see Fig. 7.5). In this instance, the pattern was achieved when the canes or threads of glass were picked up by the gather and then marvered flush with the surface. This produced a pattern in, rather than on,

7.4 Vase, transparent blue with gold spangles, h 19 cm (7³/₈ in.), glass, 18th century, coll. Alan E. Feen

7.5 Cup, colorless with 'combed' decoration, h 7 cm (2³/₄ in.), glass, 18th–19th century, coll. Mrs Barney Dagan

7.6 Low tazza, with allover opaque-white 'combed' decoration, d 19.5 cm (7³/₄ in.), glass, Venice or perhaps Tuscany, glass, late 17th–early 18th century, Christie's, London, 28 March 2000, #215

7.7 Box and cover, dark ruby-red with carved scroll and lotus pattern, d 8.6 cm (3³/₈ in.), glass, 18th century, private coll.

the surface; Venetian glass of this type is often described as combed (see Fig. 7.6). Other parallels have been drawn between the Chinese use of the 'backed-on' foot treatment (see Fig. 7.7), and the similar technique found on contemporary Venetian glassware. This particular type of foot – usually dish-shaped – is done by fusing a lump of molten glass onto the base of the object and then shaping it into the desired form.

A considerable amount of this 'influence' might be traceable to Chinese artisans having direct access to Venetian glass. The presentation of these wares at the court in Beijing can be found in documents dating back to the Yuan, Ming, and Qing periods.[17] A prime example of this is the previously mentioned *cristalli de Venezia* proffered by Mezzabarba. They comprised glass, 'some ruby color, some the color of topazes, and some the color of opals', covered bowls and cups with diamond point engraved patterns and examples of *filigrana* glass – that is, glass which contained opaque bands of white enamel.[18]

From the references thus far examined, we can see that the Kangxi era was a period of innovation in the manufacture of Chinese glass and enamel. The lack of reliable, documented pieces is a problem, and an enigma. Many of the attributions for glass from this period have been based on conjecture and 'feel'. Those pieces which have been assigned a Kangxi date bear little resemblance to the ones mentioned in contemporary records, leaving one to wonder as to their ultimate fate. Given these mitigating factors, perhaps we should reassess the inventory of early eighteenth century glass.

NOTES
1. Rosso (1984), pp. 385–7
2. Bibliotheca Apostolica Vaticana, Collezione Cinese 511 (6). See also, Rosso, pp. 835–7
3. Witek (1999), pp. 336–7
4. ARSI Jap/Sin 184, 39f–40v, 16 October 1729. Kangxi had on previous occasions raised a Jesuit to the rank of a mandarin for a particular mission
5. Loehr (1963), p. 57
6. Foucquet's 'Diary', Bibliotheca Apostolica Vaticana, Collezione Borgia, Latino, 565, pp. 112–21
7. Ibid., *Catalogue des présents envoies par l'empereur de la China – au roy* [sic] *de Portugal*, 121v.–122
8. Witek (1982), pp. 254–5
9. Plesch (1980), p. 58, Fig. 14
10. Yang Boda (1987), p. 62
11. Lam (1993), no. 12. For an example, see Kwan (2001), p. 411, #212
12. Honey (1937), pp. 211–13, 216–19, and 221–3
13. Brill (1975), pp. 121–34
14. Biblioteca Nacional de Lisboa, Fondo Gesuitico 178, 26v
15. Archives jésuites de la province de Paris, Fondo Brotier, 149, 172f, 12 November 1738. Letter by Antoine Gaubil, S. J.
16. Yang Boda (1987), p. 11
17. Marignolli's arrival in Bejing with *des verreries . . . venise*, 1342; two prisms of Venetian glass were among the gifts destined for the Wanli emperor (ARSI Jap./Sin 126, 178f–179f, 20 July 1601); Dutch ambassador's presentation of 'three goblets of Venice glass', 1656
18. APF: Scritture Originali della Congregazione Particolare dell' Indie e Cina, vol. 29, 1719, f139v

8

'When the Glass Is Being Made . . .'

The archives of the various workshops of the Zaobanchu (Imperial Household Department) are presently conserved in the First National Historical Archive of China in Beijing (*Zhongguo diyi lishi dang'anguan* 中國第一歷史檔案館).[1] Comprised of several thousand bound books, folios, scrolls and pamphlets, their meticulously detailed and precisely dated contents form the most complete record of all types of handicrafts fabricated in the workshops, and as such, are an invaluable resource for the study of art objects produced for the consumption of the Imperial household. They date from the first year of the Yongzheng reign (1723–35) to the late Qing dynasty; none exist for the Kangxi period.[2]

Worthy of note is that Yang Boda was the first Chinese scholar to utilize these archives in the study of court art during the Qing period. His discovery of a massive quantity of material from a vast reservoir of documents was a monumental achievement and marked a turning point for subsequent studies of eighteenth century Chinese art. For instance, from these records it was learned that a set of paintings, known as the *Twelve Beauties in the Yuanming Yuan*, and now in the collection of the Palace Museum, Beijing, were once mounted and displayed on a screen in the Shen Liu study of the Yuanming Yuan. In one of them, a woman is portrayed reading a book, with her arms resting on a table, next to a plain, red glass snuff bottle (see Fig. 8.1). The calligraphy on the paintings is in Yongzheng's hand, and signed with the sobriquet he used before assuming the throne '*Po chen jushi*' 破塵居士 ('Recluse of the dust of defeat'). Since he was made a prince in 1709 and ascended the throne in 1723, the portraits must have been painted within this fourteen year period.[3]

Other records show that in the first year of the reign, Prince Yi 怡親王 (Yinxiang 胤祥), younger brother of the emperor, submitted snuff bottles made of aventurine glass, five-color glass, and a red glass one decorated with enamels.[4] On the basis of this archival material it appears also that the method used to manufacture enamel wares was not yet fully under control and that a certain amount of expertise was still lacking. In the second month, fourth day, 1724, Prince Yi handed over five white porcelain cups with instructions to decorate them with enamel. Two of the pieces were broken during the firing process, and it was only

8.1 Woman reading a book, from *Twelve Beauties in the Yuanming Yuan*, h 184.6 cm
(72⅝ in.), ink and color on silk, 1709–23, Palace Museum, Beijing

8.3 Base mark, 8.2

8.2 Vase, pale celadon, with long cylindrical neck, base inscribed *Yongzheng nianzhi*, h 22.7 cm (8⁷/₈ in.), glass, 1723–35, coll. Franz

by exercising the utmost care that the enamel decor on the remaining three was successfully completed.[5] Further evidence appears in a memorial sent by Nian Gengyao 年羹堯, after the arrival of newly produced enameled peacock-feather holders on the ninth day of the second month (1724). In thanking the emperor, Nian wrote: 'The delicate, beautiful colors leave me unable to conquer my envy . . . beseeching Your saintly benevolence, if there be more enameled objects, to bestow one or two upon me in order to appease Your minion's greed.' On the back of this memorial Yongzheng wrote: 'Though I have not yet had the spare time to see to it that the enamel wares produced are of superior quality, I am confident that in the future there will be some worth seeing. For the moment I am sending you some already on hand. However, if you had not used the word "greed" I would not have given you any. It is only through your choice of wording that I grant you these pieces.'[6]

At the time the emperor gave these as-yet unperfected enamel wares to Nian, the workshop was operating with native personnel alone, and totally dependent on foreign sources for the supply of enamel colors. Craftsmen at the Imperial glassworks were directed to undertake an all-out effort towards an independent manufacture of enamel colors. According to a missive from the Yuanming Yuan 圓明園, in the seventh month of 1728, Prince Yi presented nine newly made enamels in 'colors such as soft white, yellow-brown, muted yellow, lilac, light green, dark reddish brown, deep purple, bronze and greenish-yellow. Furthermore, 'Director Hai Wang 海望 was informed by Prince Yi as follows: the [foreign] color material stored in the workshop should be used as samples; when the glass is being made, use these as standards, and order Song Qige 宋七格 to go to the glass factory and make three hundred jin 斤 [catties] of each color.'[7] Afterwards, the palace sent some of the enamel colors created in the glass factory to the superintendent of the Imperial porcelain factory at Jingdezhen 景德鎮, and Chinese painted enamel porcelain progressed to a new stage of perfection.

The archives also provide helpful information concerning the use of reign marks. In the second year (1724) of his reign, Yongzheng directed the glass workshop, 'from now on, whenever it is possible to put reign marks, such marks should be inscribed on the items' (see Fig. 8.3).[8] This practice is believed to have started during the mid to late Kangxi period, and reign marks are regarded as a characteristic feature of items coming from the Zaobanchu. Indeed, an entire hierarchy has been formulated, with yuzhi 御製, 'made by Imperial order' ranked the highest of Imperial marks, followed by the more common nianzhi 年製, 'made in', and six character marks which include the name of the dynasty, that are usually placed at the lower end of the scale. It may be remarked that examples of each type can be found on glassware in the collection of the Palace Museum, Beijing, and that reign marks on glass, like those on ceramics and jade, are notoriously unreliable.

Yongzheng established a branch of the Imperial glassworks as part of the Liusuo 六所 (six workshops) at the Yuanming Yuan in 1728. This must have occurred prior to the third month, nineteenth day, of that year, when Hai Wang brought an Imperial command for glass to be produced at the new branch at the Yuanming Yuan. The workshop was to make copies of a glass chrysanthemum dish, in fifteen different colors, two of each color.[9] Despite this, as witnessed by contemporary and archival records, the atelier established on Canchikou in 1696, does not seem to have stopped production because of this new workshop.

In January 2000, a joint project was inagurated between the Art Museum, The Chinese University of Hong Kong, and the First National Archive of China, to publish the complete set of archives related to the Zaobanchu dating from the Yongzheng to the Xuantong reigns. During the course of preparing these documents for publication, Peter Lam observed that the records for the Zaobanchu utilized two official names for the Imperial glassworks, i.e. *bolichang* 玻璃廠 (glass factory), and *bolizuo* 玻璃作 (glass workshop). At first this was treated as either a careless mistake or a variant in referring to the same atelier. However, with the establishment of the workshop at the Yuanming Yuan, it became apparent that *chang* 廠 (factory), and *zuo* 作 (workshop) referred to two, different, contemporary units within the Imperial glassworks. Confirmation of this came to light when in two instances these variants appeared on the same archival document. The first document dated tenth day, eleventh month, fourth year Qianlong (1739), begins with an edict from the glass workshop (*zuo*) saying, 'To coincide with the New Year's festival ask the glass factory (*chang*) to present sixty snuff bottles.' Following the same form, the second one, dated eighth day, fifth month, sixth year Qianlong, the glass workshop asked the glass factory to make several sets of chessmen. As to differentiating between the two, by taking into consideration all of the documentation pertaining to the Imperial glassworks, and the personal habits of the emperors, Peter Lam proposed that it was not unreasonable to suggest that *bolizuo* was used to denote the glass workshop at the Yuanming Yuan, and *bolichang* referred to the original atelier on Canchikou.[10] This is certainly compatible with Jesuit-composed Chinese language dictionaries, where the character *chang* (factory) was invariably used to define a glass workshop.

Records related to the original glass workshop (*chang*) note in the fifth year (1727), third month, thirteenth day, of Yongzheng, Prince Yi sent an order for the glassworks to copy a small glass cup with red overlay (*tao* 套) on a yellow ground. Zhao Zhiqian's (趙之謙) treatise on glass, *Notes Written at Leisure in Yonglu* (*Yonglu xianjie* 勇盧閒詰), states that glass overlays in diverse forms and motifs had already been made during Kangxi's reign. However, Zhao's work was written and published in the late nineteenth century, and no confidently dated specimen for this period has as yet been identified.

Overlay or cased glass consists of two or more layers of different colors, with the outer layer usually carved on a wheel to reveal the lower or inside layer. This technique of 'cameo cutting' was well known to Chinese lapidary craftsmen and it found a new outlet with the introduction of overlay or cased glass. The few

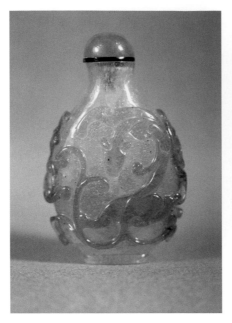

8.4 Snuff bottle, single overlay of pale blue on bubble ground, carved in relief with design of four *chilong*, 6.8 cm (2⁵/₈ in.), glass, 18th–19th century, private coll.

8.6 Jar, with dotted shades pink, blue and white between two transparent layers, h 9.9 cm (3⁷/₈ in.), glass; attributed to 18th century, private coll.

8.5 Rython, variegated blue, carved in relief with design of *chilong*, h 12 cm (4⁵/₈ in.), glass, 18th century, coll. Alan E. Feen

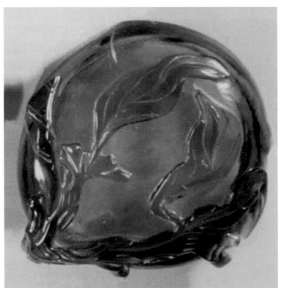

8.7 One of a pair of amber-colored peach form boxes, with relief carving, d 8.9 cm (3¹/₂ in.), glass, 18th century, coll. Alan E. Feen

8.8 Cup, one of original ten, swirled red and orange simulating realgar, h 3.5 cm (1⁵/₈ in.), glass, before 1732, The National Museum of Denmark, Department of Ethnography, EBc71–82. Photographer: Lennart Larsen

8.9 Pair of vases, faceted purse-shaped, mottled red and orange simulating realgar, h 15.8 cm (6³/₈ in.), glass, first half of the 18th century, coll. Shuisongshi Shanfang

examples which are registered in the archives for the Yongzheng period may not constitute a major line of production, but they do provide firm evidence for the use of this type of decoration. In addition to the example cited above, records of the Zaobanchu for the second month, ninth and tenth days, 1726, note the completion of one pair of blue overlay *chi* 螭 dragon snuff bottles (see Fig. 8.4), and an order in the ninth month, twenty-third day, 1726, makes mention of a red glass overlay jar for which a gold cover had been ordered.[11] The subsequent completion of the cover was itself noted on the twenty-fourth day of the following month.

The entry for the decor on the snuff bottles reads *chihu*, i.e. dragon-tiger (虎), which has provoked some discussion as to the probability of a tiger as part of the design. This would render the translation of the phrase as '*chi*-dragon decoration', somewhat inaccurate. However, a *chilong* (dragon) has been defined as: one which has a head like a tiger's, a slim body without scales, and a forked tail. Tigers are rarely pictured on snuff bottles; several reasons are given for this, the principle one being their association with the inauspicious aspect of the Yin 陰 element in the universe. The tiger was symbolically a personification of the Yin − since it was a creature of the night that slunk silently through the forests in search of its prey.[12] These fanciful animals also appear commonly as the principle motif on cups and vases, sometimes with one running up each side (see Fig. 8.5), and/or with their bodies arched out to serve as handles.

In as much as the Qing royal family belonged to the yellow sect of Lama Buddhism, the glassworks furnished beads and bowls for use in their worshiping halls, and also served an important mission by providing bestowal gifts for the emperor. One memorandum notes that the gifts intended for an ambassador from the Dalai Lama are three pairs of glass bowls with covers, one pair of glass dishes, and one pair of glass vases. Other records note the order of both green and yellow glass Buddhist beads, and an Imperial command to the glassworks (*bolichang*), to make yellow, blue, and golden-yellow glass sacral bowls copying the Yixing-bowl style. Samples of the bowls were ordered for approval. They were completed in the fifth month, twenty-fifth day, 1733.[13]

The enormous volume of output for glass objects during Yongzheng's thirteen year reign, is given as close to one thousand items. From the archives, it is known that glass production reached its highest volume between the fifth and seventh years of the reign. Objects were produced in monchromes, others decorated with overlays, enameling, engraving and gold painting. There were bottles, vases, jars, washers, covered boxes, waste jars (*zhadou* 渣斗), bowls, flowerpots, brush holders, shallow bowls, daily utensils, and items for the scholar's desk. A dozen glass vessels with incised Yongzheng reign marks, can be found in the collection of the Palace Museum, Beijing. They range in color from all shades of yellow, to bright blue, and purple. The emperor seems to have had a preference for red and purple, although the snuff bottle he is alleged to have used was a glass one in sapphire blue.

This leaves one to speculate on the disposition of the twenty 'blue sky after rain' (*tianqing* 天晴) colored glass snuff bottles which were recorded as 'completed' on the twenty-first day, second month, fourth year (1726) of Yongzheng's reign. A previous attempt to duplicate this color had not been successful. Apparently, this problem was soon overcome, for in addition to the snuff bottles we find records for an order and the completion of a 'blue sky after rain' glass jar of bundle shape, painted with a continuous design of gold flowers. A similar set of records show in 1735 twenty-five glass water-pots and ten glass brush-rests were made in five different colors: red, yellow, pale green, 'blue sky after rain' (*tianqing*), and sky-blue (*tianlan* 天藍).[14]

Mention should be made of the ten glass wine cups which were brought from Guangzhou (Canton) in 1732 on the *Kronprins Christian*. They are now in the collection of the Royal Danish Kunstkammer. When first catalogued in 1737, the cups were described as 'twelve small teacups made of prepared agate in China, some are yellow on the inside and red-brown on the outside, and yellow enameled' (see Fig. 8.8).[15] Variegated orange, or frequently red and orange, glass was extremely popular during the Qing dynasty. It imitates the poisonous mineral realgar (arsenic sulphide, *xionghuang* 雄黄), an importance substance in Daoist alchemical practice. Since the material itself is soft and prone to disintegrate into powder – thus, potentially lethal – a glass substitute was utilized. The Palace Museum, Beijing, possesses other Yongzheng period examples of realgar glass,[16] and the British Museum's founding collection, which dates from before 1753, includes realgar glass cups, and a pair of faceted bundle-shaped vases (for another pair, see Fig. 8.9).

Yongzheng craftsmen may not have added anything new to glassmaking techniques, but they did their work skillfully and by carrying forward what had been accomplished in the past, set a standard for their successors to follow.

NOTES

1. Yang Boda (1983), pp. 13–16, and Lam (2000), pp. 46–7
2. Lam (2000), p. 46
3. Tian Jiaqing (1993), p. 32
4. Zhang Rong (2000), p. 65
5. Zhu Jiajin (1982), p. 67, no. 1
6. See, *Wenxian congbian*, (ed.) National Palace Museum, repr. Taipei, 1964, pp. 859–60. *Gongzhong dang Yongzheng chao zou zhe*, (ed.) National Palace Museum, Taipei, 1977, vol. 1, pp. 829–30
7. Zhu Jiajin (1982), p. 67, no. 2 & 3; p. 69, no. 4 & no. 11; p. 71, no. 7
8. Lam (2000), p. 50
9. Zhang Rong (2000), p. 62
10. Lam (2000), p. 48
11. Zhang Rong (2000), pp. 64, 65
12. See Cammann (1982), pp. 16–18
13. Zhang Rong (2000), pp. 66–7
14. Archives no. 3294, Yang Boda (1987), p. 62; Zhang Rong (2000), pp. 61, 63, 65
15. Hardie (1990), p. 21, White (1992), p. 13
16. Yang Boda (1983), p. 10

9.1 Faceted vase, opaque yellow, base inscribed *Qianlong nianzhi*, h 14.2 cm (5¹/₂ in.), glass, 1736−95, coll. Franz

9

Glass: The Yellow of a Broom Flower

Glassmaking thrived during the reign of the Qianlong emperor (*r.*1736–1795), and is considered to have reached its zenith from the fifth to the twenty-fourth years of his reign. Palace records show that in 1740, two Jesuit missionaries joined the Imperial glass workshops.[1] They were Gabriel-Léonard de Brossard (*Ji Wen* 紀文) and Pierre d'Incarville (*Tang Zhizhong* 湯執中). Prior to his departure for China, d'Incarville had 'worked for many months in a glass workshop at Rouen.' This workshop can be identified as the royal glassworks on rue du Pré, in Saint-Sever parish, Rouen. D'Incarville learned the methods employed there from the master glass craftsman, Antoine-François Hubert.[2] Brossard, was presumably a member of a distinguished family of '*Gentilhommes Verriers*', whose glassmaking activities can be traced back to the seventeenth century. The archives record their production of aventurine and blue glass,[3] and suggest that in addition to working at the glassworks (*bolichang*) on Canchikou, they worked, at least some of the time, at the Yuanming Yuan workshop (*bolizuo*).

An indication as to the efforts they expended to make these various types of glass appear in a series of letters d'Incarville sent to his sister, Marie-Madeleine Rondeaux. On 20 September 1742, d'Incarville asked her 'to direct my brother d'Epreville to obtain for us from the good lady Massolet the secrets of the glassworks which are presently not essential to them.' D'Incarville concluded his letter of 6 October the same year by asking his sister if she could find out from the glassworks in Rouen, how to make aventurine, and a glass that he described as being the color of a yellow broom flower.[4]

D'Incarville had experienced great difficulties in his attempts to make aventurine glass,[5] and his own account is contained in a small dictionary he entrusted, apparently in 1748, to the care of the Russian caravans from Kiaktha (resp. Moscow), which visited Beijing on a tri-annual basis. The manuscript was eventually published by Aleksei Kirillovich Razumovskii, president of Moscow's Imperial Society of Naturalists, under the title *Catalogue alphabétique des plantes et autre objets d'historie naturelle en usage en Chine*. It offers a rewarding insight into the methods employed at the Imperial glassworks.

Antimony   If there is any in China, they are not aware of it.

Borax   It is not very expensive in Beijing. They use it as in Europe, to consolidate in glass, and in medicine.

Crystal   It is new to China. What they are presently making is beautiful. The composition [for it] is not as simple as ours. It lacks magnesia.

Glass   That of China, called liuli is not made at all from rice cinders, as it has been said by some authors. It is composed of flint, saltpeter, and tsee che [sic., white arsenic].

Verdigris   It is used to give the color green to glass.[6]

Yellow was the color reserved for the use of the Imperial family and certain other high officials, hence d'Incarville's interest in making a shade comparable to that found on the yellow broom flower. Compounds of antimony can be used for the color yellow, and although there are extensive deposits of it in China, principally in the ore Stibnite, as d'Incarville noted, it was not used for this purpose. A list of the cost of material for the Zaobanchu for 1753 included borax (*pengsha* 硼砂), which, the Chinese claimed, was a feature of western glass, and also that its use had been introduced by the missionaries.[7]

Of coal d'Incarville reported: 'It enters into Beijing each day in an almost unbelievable quantity . . . There is a special type used for the smithy which has a lot of activity (*activité*), one needs to use a bellows in order to kindle it, and to maintain it. That which is used to cast iron, . . . needs so much from the bellows that the workers cannot sustain the fumes. The kind, which is used in Beijing to make glass, has more activity than the ordinary [type].'[8]

Production of glass articles is dependent upon several crucial steps. It begins with batch mixing of raw materials and their melting. After it has melted, the molten glass, called metal, is held for a time at a high temperature for refining, which removes bubbles and streaks. The temperature is then slowly reduced so that the viscosity of the batch makes it suitable for forming, after which the glass must be slowly cooled or annealed, usually in a long oven called a *lehr*. Considering the importance of these steps, and d'Incarville's comments, it is apparent that the glass-workers had difficulty in sustaining consistent furnace temperatures due to the coal's 'somewhat unpredictable burning rate.'[9] There were occasional exceptions. In 1782 and 1783, Qianlong ordered that the wood-blocks from books ranked as *jinshu* 禁書 (forbidden books), were to be used as fuel for the glass furnaces. This was considered to be the most suitable and confidential way to dispose of them.[10]

The flower of the *haitang* 海棠 tree (*Pyrus spectabilis*), a variety of the crab apple, figured in Chinese decorative motifs. It was considered highly auspicious because its color, red, was the Chinese color for happiness, and it was also popular because the second syllable of its name made a pun on another word also pronounced *tang*. This made it suitable for inclusion among rebus pictures especially, to illustrate the auspicious phrase *jinyou mangtang* 金玉茫堂 (a hall filled

9.2 Candle holder, red over cream and bright yellow ring socket, inscribed *Qianlong nianzhi*, d 18 cm (7 in.), glass, 1736–95, coll. William Lillyman, photograph by Ognan Borissov

9.3 Brush-handle, ruby-red on snowflake ground with raised *Daqing Qianlong fanggu* mark, l 15.5 cm (6 in.), glass, 1736–95, coll. William Lillyman, photograph by Ognan Borissov

with gold and jade).[11] The blossom is regularly represented with four petals, of which the upper and lower ones are short and round, while those extending to the right and left are very much longer. By this shape we can identify the *haitang* blossom as a fairly common subject for the metal guard-plates on toggles, and its more scarce appearance on glass. The yellow *gaidou* 蓋豆 (hemispherical fruit bowl with high stem and spreading foot) in the collection of the Palace Museum, Beijing, is overlaid with red designs of the Chinese character *shou* 壽 (longevity).[12] Alert observers will single out the *haitang* blossoms which adorn the foot rim. A glass candle holder may be an even more unusual example (see Fig. 9.2). It is well-carved, through the red overlay to the cream-colored body, with a design of four archaistic dragons around the everted rim. The cavetto has four detached *haitang*

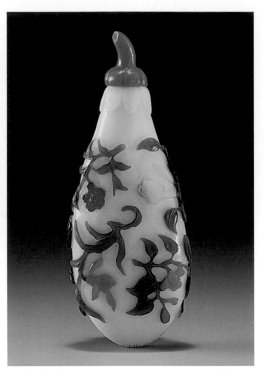

9.5 Snuff bottle, multi-color overlay on white, carved with nine different flowers, *Qianlong yuzhi* seal mark on base, h 7.5 cm (2⁷/₈ in.), glass, photograph courtesy of Robert Hall

9.4 Vase, *gu*-form, carved red over snowflake with peony and acanthus leaves, h 14.6 cm (5³/₄ in.), glass, attributed to 18th century, courtesy Weisbrod Chinese Art Ltd

9.6 Covered box, clear with blue and gold enamel with design of branches and berries, *Qianlong ninazhi* mark on base, d 6 cm (2³/₈ in.), glass, 1736–95, coll. Shuisongshi Shangfang

blossoms borne on foliate and scrolling vines divided by *ruyi* 如意 heads, all encircling a central dome carved with lappets and a bright yellow ring socket. An incised four-character Qianlong mark is evenly spaced around the underside.

In the third month, twelfth day of 1753, Qianlong ordered a group of glass pieces to be boxed together *baishijian* 百什件 – literally '100 pieces' but meaning specially fitted boxes for a series of small treasures, also known as *duobaoge* 多寶格.[13] The group included two wine-yellow glass seals; one set of yellow glass scroll-pins; four chrysanthemum dishes; some *clair de lune* glass beads; an aventurine-glass handled peace-chariot; a *clair de lune* glass small, round incense burner; a transparent blue glass snuff bottle with silver mounts; a green aventurine-glass snuff bottle, and a white glass gourd-shaped snuff bottle. The following year, the emperor ordered two blue glass dishes of different sizes to be stored together with other miniature pieces in curio boxes.[14] One of these boxes in the collection of National Palace Museum, Taipei, contains five rare glass curios fashioned in the form of traditional Manchurian toys known as 'Galahas' – a word which refers to small pieces of bone in the legs of pigs or lambs. Manchurian girls dyed *Galahas* different colors and threw them for fun.[15]

Enameled glassware of the Qianlong period is noted for its refinement. A file dated to 1738 records an order for the glass workshop (*bolichang*) to make various pieces including an enameled 'vase in brocade bundle shape'.[16] There are two possible candidates for this description. The first is a pouch-shaped vase realistically carved with a pink sash at the neck, and enameled to simulate an Imperial-yellow brocade which has been decorated with twelve shaded blue foliate *chilong* (see Fig. 9.7), while the second example is superbly painted in *famille rose* palette on each side with a phoenix swooping from lavender, blue and pink clouds to a bed of tree peonies (see Fig. 9.8).[17]

Brossard's carved glass and enamels adorned the throne room in Beijing, where they were extolled as rivaling the most exquisite and beautiful objects sent from France and England.[18] The Imperial archives recorded that from the eleventh month, twentieth day, to the third month, sixteenth day of 1753, Brossard succeeded in producing ('firing'): three glass floral groups in imitation European style; nine glass lanterns; eight glass basins; two glass pitchers; three threaded glass pitchers, and one threaded glass cylindrical brush pot.[19] They include also orders to the workshop that the pitchers are to be kept, together with their originals, 'until the carved decoration is finished', and to 'make a few similar fine pitchers next year.' Additionally, since the original furnace for making large pieces had become unusable, a new furnace was built to accommodate them. In 1754, the emperor gave instructions that two sets of glass ornamental groups which had been made by Brossard, were to be displayed at the Qianqing Palace 乾清宮 for the New Year Festival.

The missionaries were then in the midst of constructing a series of European palaces and gardens for the Yuanming Yuan. Many of the items adorning this complex were furnished by the Imperial glassworks. Records for the fifth month,

9.7 Vase, pouch-shaped, with foliate *chilong*, painted enamels on white ground, *Qianlong nianzhi* mark on body, h 18.8 cm (7³/₈ in.), glass, 1736–95, Sotheby's, Hong Kong, 15 November 1988, #77

9.8 Vase modeled as a brocade bag, painted enamels on milk-white ground, *Qianlong nianzhi* mark on body, h 18.2 cm (7¹/₈ in.), glass, 1736–95, Sotheby's, Hong Kong, 15 November 1988, #75

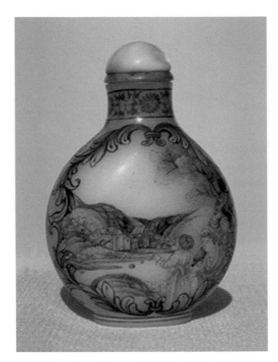

9.9 Snuff bottle with European figures in
landscape, painted enamels on white,
base inscribed *Qianlong nianzhi*, h 4.3 cm
(1⁵/₈ in.), glass, 1736–95, coll. M. M. Young

thirteenth day, 1753, noted: 'On the altar table at the western platform of the
Fountain Hall [in the western-style palace at the Yuanming Yuan], a pair of glass
lanterns should be added. Ask Lang Shining 郎世寧 [Giuseppe, Castiglione, S. J.]
to produce a design for my approval.' Castiglione submitted two designs on the
fifteenth day (1753). They were approved, and further instructions given that
the materials and artisans needed to execute them should be requested through
the Zaobanchu. In the tenth month, seventeenth day, 1754, four gold-star glass
stem cups on silver dishes, with reign marks inscribed, were presented to Qianlong.
He ordered them to be displayed in the Fountain Hall (*Shuifa* 水法).[20] In 1756, the
emperor ordered four pairs of multi-colored glass lanterns in imitation of the
imported ones hanging in the hallways of the Fountain Hall. Castiglione took charge
of the design and Brossard acted as technical director in their manufacture.[21]

After d'Incarville's death in 1757, and Brossard's in 1758, glassmaking at the
Imperial workshop is considered to have entered a period of decline. In the second
month, seventh day, 1759, the glass workshop (*bolichang*) submitted three sets of
three-colored glass pieces described as 'five offerings'. They displeased the
emperor, who instructed that no charge should be made, and that their cost should
be ascertained and repaid by those responsible.[22] In the twenty-fifth year (1760)
Qianlong, to his disappointment, learned that there were no longer any missionaries
at court who were skilled in the techniques of glassblowing.[23] These, and other
incidents, indicate that western missionaries were no longer attached to the

9.10 Pair of vases, painted enamels on opaque white, base inscribed *Qianlong nianzhi*, h 16.2 cm (6³/₈ in.), glass, probably 1736–95, The Corning Museum of Glass, Corning, NY, Anonymous gift, No. 53.6.1.

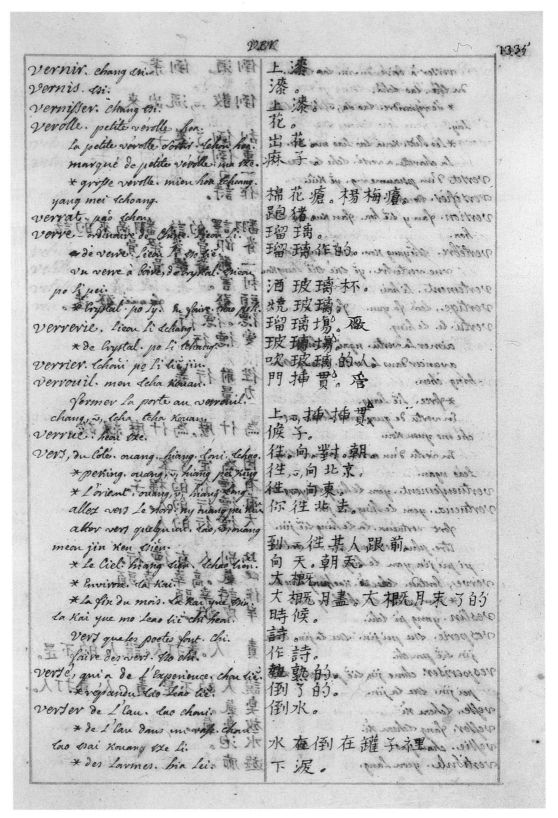

9.11 Extract, d'Incarville's *Dictionnaire français-chinois* with the Chinese terms for glass, etc., photographic reproduction by the Bibliothèque nationale de France, Ms Chinois 9277

Imperial glass workshops, and point to general a lack of skilled glassblowers. The records of the Zaobanchu contain entries for glassware through the final year of Qianlong's reign, so that any decrease in production might simply have been due to waning interest by the emperor.

Pierre d'Incarville and Gabriel Léonard de Brossard were associated with Imperial glassmaking for more than fifteen years. The glassware made during their tenure at the workshops covers a wide range of shapes and a dazzling variety and combination of colors. Their legacy is contained in the glass they helped to make and to some extent in d'Incarville's *Dictionnaire français-chinois*. This beautiful manuscript, presently conserved in the Bibliothèque Nationale, consists of some 1185 pages, with the Chinese characters rendered in d'Incarville's own hand (see Fig. 9.11). While the full circumstances of its passage from China to Paris are unknown, it is clear that it came into the possession of Sir George Staunton while he was in China with the Macartney embassy of 1793–4. Staunton brought the manuscript back to England, where it remained undetected among his papers until 1866.[24] Perhaps, the most noteworthy aspect of it is, that it provides the Chinese terms then in use for glass (*liuli*), crystal (*poli*), and the glassworks (*liuli chang*), etc., by a European who actually had made glass in the Imperial workshop.

NOTES
1. Archives, no. 3399, Yang Boda (1983), p. 16, #47
2. Bibliothèque Nationale, N.A.F. 6556, 13 October 1739, f26v–f27, letter by Jean-Baptiste DuHalde. His proper name was Pierre Le Chéron, to which he added d'Incarville, the name of a fief near Louviers, where he was born
3. Archives, nos 3395 & 3392, Yang Boda (1983), p. 16, #48, & #49
4. Verdier (1904), pp. 73–9
5. 'Catalogue alphabétique', vol. 3, p. 112
6. 'Catalogue alphabétique', vol. 3, pp. 103 & 128; vol. 4, pp. 37 & 85–6
7. Zhang Weiyong (2000), p. 75
8. 'Catalogue alphabétique', vol. 3, pp. 126–7
9. Morache (1869), pp. 41–2
10. Lam, (2000), p. 49
11. Cammann (1962), pp. 107–108 & 246
12. Zhang Weiyong (2000), p. 75
13. Archives, no. 3444, Lam (2000), pp. 23 & 56, and Zhang, Weiyong, p. 74
14. Archives, no. 3443, Lam (2000), pp. 50–51
15. For illustrations see: *The National Palace Museum Monthly of Chinese Art*, Taipei, 1985, vol. 33, p. 10
16. Archives, no. 3382, Lam (2000), p. 52
17. *The Paul and Helen Bernat Collection of Important Qing Imperial Porcelain and Works of Art*, Sotheby's, Hong Kong, 15 November, 1988, #75, & #77
18. Rochemontiex, P. Camille de (1915), *Joseph Amiot et les derniers survivants de la mission française à Pékin*, 1750–95, Paris, p. 79
19. Archives, no. 3475, Yang Boda (1983), p. 16, #46, and Lam (2000), p. 45
20. Archives, nos 3442 & 3448, Lam (2000), pp. 49–51 & 56
21. Archives, no. 3493, Yang Boda (1983), p. 16, #53
22. Zhang Weiyong (2000), p. 73
23. Zhang Weiyong (2000), p. 75
24. For Staunton's account of the mission see *An Authentic Account of an Embassy from the King of Great Britain to the Emperor of China*, London, 1797. In 1866, the noted French Sinologist, M. G. Pauthier acquired d'Incarville's *Dictionnaire*. It is presently in the collection of the Bibliothèque Nationale, Ms Chinois 9277.

10.1 Detail, banquet held to celebrate the empress dowager's 60th birthday, 97.5 × 161.2 cm (38⅜ × 63 in.), watercolor on silk, post 1752, Palace Museum, Beijing

10

'The Harmony of the Seasons'

Emily Byrne Curtis and Ricardo Joppert, Ph.D.

A long silk hand scroll painting by court artists records various scenes from the elaborate celebration Qianlong ordered to honor his mother, Empress Dowager Xiaosheng 孝聖, on the occasion of her sixtieth birthday (1751).[1] One section of the scroll shows the decorative arches and sculptures erected along the road from the Yuanming Yuan to the Forbidden City, while another depicts the gold sedan chair carrying the empress dowager as well as her retinue of officials. The Imperial cortege passed by 'ice boats' busily engaged in the popular sport of ice racing, and the progressive action of the procession, seen as we turn our attention from one portion of the scroll to another, produces a vivid sense of motion. At the banquet held in the Palace of Benevolent Peace (*Cining Gong* 慈寧宮), the Qianlong emperor himself is depicted bringing a goblet to his mother, who as the guest of honor is seated at the dais (see Fig. 10.1).[2] A list of the gifts Xiaosheng received at this time may be found in the *Guochao gongshi* 國朝宮史 (*History of the Qing Imperial Palaces*), together with those presented on her seventieth birthday.[3]

The glasswares 'respectfully recorded'[4] on the eleventh month, twenty-fifth day, *xinwei* 辛未 year (1751):

On the twenty-second day:
'The harmony of the seasons', tall red glass candlesticks, one pair.
'Round heaven, gold *ni* 猊 beast', red glass censer, one item.
'Willow branch, to drop dew', red glass flower vases [*hua ping* 花瓶], one pair.
'Clear waves, immortal's ornament', green glass *ruyi*, set in *zitan* 紫壇 wood, one scepter.
'Morning mist, clear scenery', red glass *ruyi*, set in *zitan* wood, one scepter.
'Brilliant, five color', glass vessels, 99 [pieces].

On the twenty-fourth day:
'Liberated greatness, full brightness', white glass table lanterns, one pair.
'The moon dispenses reflections', glass mirrors, hanging, 9 pieces.

On the twenty-fifth day:
'Dew hands, high raised', white glass tumblers, tall, one pair.

'Jade fingers, sweat of clouds', white glass cups, one pair.

'Smoky mist disperses benevolence', glass wine cups with engraved flower pattern,
one pair.

'Glow of colors, jade handle', goblets with handles and engraved flower pattern,
6 pairs.

In the *xinsu* 辛酉 year (1761) of Qianlong – for the empress dowager's seventieth birthday celebrations – she received:

On the twenty-second day:

'Precious pearls to the fullness', white glass *ruyi* set in *zitan* wood, one scepter.

'Green river Han, vast light', ornamental glass tablet, [framed to stand on the table],
one piece.

'Silver flowers, reflecting colors', painted glass table screen, one piece.

'Jade tower, beautiful scenery', glass table screens depicting the 'Hundred Antiquities',[5]
one pair.

'Jade sea, twilight mists over peaks', glass table screen [inlaid with lacquer] depicting the
'Isles of Immortals' supported by turtles, one piece.

'Most joyous celebration in the capital of the Immortals', auspicious glass table screen,
one piece.

'Cleaning skies over the Shanglin hunting parks in spring', glass table screen depicting
flowers and birds, one piece.

'Pure brightness shines everywhere', ornamental glass tablet [framed to stand on tables],
one piece.

On the twenty-sixth day:

'Immortal corolla, shining everywhere', ivory – inlaid glass square flower basket,
one piece.

'Rarefied clouds, five color', glass vessels, 99 [pieces].

On the twenty-seventh day:

Miniature landscape [*penjing* 盆景] in glass inside a cage for small birds, depicting
'precious birds while dancing', inlaid with *nan mu* 楠木 wood, inlaid mottled bamboo,
one piece.

On the twenty-eighth day:

'Autumn flower (beauty), golden luster', yellow [*huang* 黃] glass dishes with
chrysanthemum[6] petal pattern, 2 pieces.

'The heaven, bright and clear', white [*bai* 白] glass dish with chrysanthemum petal
pattern, one piece.

'Green wash, spring ripples', green [*lu* 綠] glass dish with chrysanthemum petal pattern,
one piece.

'The deep red gem flows with brightness', red [*hong* 紅] glass dish with chrysanthemum
petal pattern, one piece.

'The peak of west mountain, the deep blue – as of distant hills', blue [*lan* 藍] glass dish with chrysanthemum petal pattern, one piece.

'Golden waves, overwhelming, rolling and tossing of billows', yellow glass dish with chrysanthemum petal pattern, one piece.

'Reflected from the water, heaven's light', blue-green [*qing* 青] glass dish with chrysanthemum petal pattern, one piece.

'Twilight vapors descend and scatter', purple-violet [*zi* 紫] glass dish with chrysanthemum petal pattern, one piece.

'Milky way surrounds and reflects', plain, round, white glass plates, 18 pieces.

'Blue woods, jade wings', gold star [aventurine] glass mountain-shaped brush rest, one piece.

'Dragon hand, auspicious cloudy but bright sky', red glass water container, one piece.

On the twenty-ninth day:

'Ruomu, pure flowers',[7] glass table screens set in *zitan* wood, nine pieces.

'Coral frame, frozen flower', hanging glass panels [framed in] *zitan* wood inlaid with ivory, 3 pairs.

On the thirtieth day:

'Jade heaven, clear stars', gold star [aventurine] glass *ruyi*, one scepter.

A jade book in the collection of the Forbidden City records 'that in the thirty-sixth year of the reign of the emperor Qianlong (1771), he honored his mother, with a laudatory title to celebrate her eightieth birthday.'[8] According to the *Dongchao chongyang lu* 東朝崇養錄,[9] Xiaosheng was presented with a total of sixteen pieces of glass which included:

Wine [*jiu* 酒] yellow glass hand basin, one piece.

Various color glass chrysanthemum flower plates, five pieces.

Green glass, four inch [*cun* 寸] plate, one piece.

Yellow glass six-inch plate, four pieces.

Plum [*mei* 梅] blue glass five-inch plate, one piece.

Kingfisher [*feicui* 翡翠] color glass five-inch plate, one piece.

Green threaded glass six-inch plate, one piece.

Golden yellow glass five-inch plate, one piece.

Grape [*pu* 葡]color glass five-inch plate, one article.

As mentioned, (see Chapter 8), in 1728, Xiaosheng's consort, the Yongzheng emperor had sent to the glass workshop (*bolichang*) a lacquer plate with chrysanthemum shape and gilt decoration from the Jiajing period (1522–66). He ordered the glassworks to copy it, and to make, by winter, a few sets of the dish in the same size, but without its decoration. Each set was to be comprised of fifteen or twenty pieces, in an equal number of different colors. The workshop seems to have filled this order, for we find a record in the third month, twenty-second day,

1728, that it was to copy the glass chrysanthemum dish as before, but to make it smaller. Thirty pieces were ordered, of fifteen different colors with two of each color. The emperor then told them precisely how and where to display them in a particular pavilion, on a small lacquer display shelf in six groups of five pieces each.[10] According to other archival records, the four chrysanthemum dishes Qianlong ordered to be boxed together in 1753, were made of aventurine glass.[11]

There is, in Chinese, a complex vocabulary containing tonal subtleties that permit rich variations in meaning. Basically a composite color, zi 紫 is a blend of red and blue which gives the violet on purple. It evokes a group of stars next to the Polar Star, called ziweiyuan 紫微垣 'The Wall of Purple Tenuity', the site of Shangdi's (上帝) palace, the ziweigong 紫微宮.[12] Its parallel on earth is the Purple Forbidden City, Zijincheng 紫禁城.[13] Additional refinements are suggested by the descriptive phrases preceding the colors. By itself, xia 霞 can refer to rosy clouds, the mist in daybreak or twilight, and so forth. However, in the context of the phrase 'morning mist', xia evokes the red sky in the morning – therefore red vapors, thus adding a further dimension to the color of the red glass in the ruyi scepter. This not only adds to the visual imagery, but alludes to important literary and iconographical connotations to a ruler's enlightened government.[14]

Given that Xiaosheng followed the precepts of Buddha, it is possible that some of the gifts of glass were intended as a subtle allusion to her status as a mother/deity figure. For instance, in addition to being an important emblem of rank, the ruyi scepter (see Fig. 10.5) was also as a symbol of Buddha and his doctrines. Thus, the glass ruyi scepters presented to Xiaosheng can be related to Buddhism on two levels – symbolic and material.

Qianlong claimed that the purpose of much of the building at the Changchun Yuan 長春園 was to prepare for his retirement in life (see Fig. 10.9). Construction of one of his pavilions, the Jian Yuan 鑒園 (Garden of Reflection) was completed in 1767. Some two hundred years later, this site provided the answer to a term which had long puzzled scholars. The term Guyue Xuan 古月軒 (Ancient Moon Pavilion) had been applied somewhat indiscriminately to describe a small group of Imperial porcelain and glass of the finest quality. However, it was difficult to attribute to such marked pieces to the workshops of the Zaobanchu, since none of the buildings in the Imperial palaces bore the name Guyue Xuan. This led to the formulation of several, carefully constructed hypotheses, based primarily on the components found in the character for 'hu' 胡. Ceramic specialists eventually concluded that it might be best to discontinue use of the term, and, in fact, began to do so, but the issue was still unresolved for the small glass objects with this mark (see Figs. 10.10, 10.11).

This predicament was resolved when, in 1981, two architects He Chongyi and Zeng Zhaofen, began to publish the results of their research project on restoring the Yuanming Yuan. Their most important finding was an entry of 'Guyue Xuan' in the Jian Yuan.[15] From this, and other sources it was learned that the Jian Yuan

10.3 Base mark, 10.2

10.2 Vase, transparent red, base incised *Qianlong nianzhi*, 22 cm (8⁵/₈ in.), glass, 1736–95, coll. Franz

10.4 'Chrysanthemum' dish, molded with forty-eight petals, bright primrose yellow, base incised *Qianlong nianzhi*, d 17.8 cm (7 in.), glass, 1736–95, photograph courtesy of Sotheby's, London

10.5 *Ruyi* scepter with *lingzi*, translucent green, l approx. 20.5 cm (8 in.), glass, Qing dynasty, (1644–1912), coll. Ina and Sandford Gadient

10.7 Shallow bowl, opaque yellow, base incised *Qianlong nianzhi*, h 4.3 cm (1³/₈ in.), glass, 1736–95, coll. Franz

10.6 Paperweight, carved red over yellow, with dragon, clouds and wave pattern, *Qianlong nianzhi* mark on base, h 6.4 cm (2¹/₂ in.), glass, late 18th–early 19th century, private coll.

10.8 Bowl, the exterior cut with register of facets, transparent amethyst, *Qianlong ninazhi* mark on base, h 7 cm (2³/₄ in.), glass, 18th century, Suntory Museum of Art, Tokyo

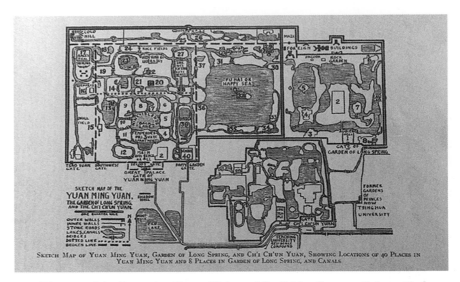

10.9 Diagram of the Yuanming Yuan, *History of the Peking Summer Palaces Under the Ch'ing Dynasty*, Carroll Brown Malone, 1936

was situated in the southeastern corner of the Changchung Yuan, stretched along the edge of a lake (see Fig. 10.12). Its main hall, the Airan Jingyun 藹然靜雲, was linked up with covered corridors to various buildings. Guyue Xuan was located at the back of the main hall and was five columns in width.[16]

It has been proposed that Qianlong might have ordered the glassware with a Guyue Xuan mark for use in this garden.[17] In 1771, he composed a poem about the Jian Yuan, and described the garden as being surrounded by water which was clean and clear, and that, when viewed from mirrors in the pavilion, the whole area was like glass. The length of time that the Imperial workshops continued to make Guyue Xuan marked pieces is uncertain, but some time during the nineteenth century, copies made outside the palace began to appear, which brings up the following points for consideration.

Jean Joseph-Marie Amiot's, S. J. (Qian Deming 錢德明) description of status for the Imperial glassworks in 1775, begins by recalling that the first workshop had been established in Beijing, by a religious person, during the reign of Kangxi. Now, however, 'the Emperor has not even taken the trouble to assign apprentices to the European glassmakers, or even to have glassworkers transferred from Canton.'[18] His somewhat gloomy assessment is correct in that it points out the diminishing production at the Imperial glassworks (*bolichang*). Boshan had fully regained its status as one of China's most important glassmaking centers, and private workshops in Beijing are credited with having made wonderfully decorated items of glassware in gem tones. It is possible that another reason for the decline of production at the Imperial glassworks was that Beijing and Boshan artisans had begun to fill orders for the palace.

The Palace Museum, Beijing possesses several hundred examples of glass vessels from this period. Hundreds more have been given a Qianlong attribution,

10.10 Water pot, painted enamels on white, markon *Guyue xuan* base, h 6 cm (2³/₈ in.), glass, 18th–19th century, Sotheby's, Hong Kong, 15 November 1988, #74

10.11 Detail of a *Guyue xuan* mark

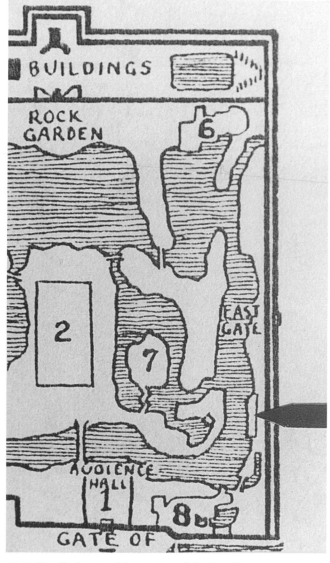

10.12 Detail of 10.9 with location of the Jian Yuan

10.13 Raspberry over clear snowflake and green color cicada and lotus leaf, l 4.8 cm (1⁷/₈ in.), glass, late 18th–early 19th century, coll. Alan E. Feen

10.14 Gourd-shape bottle with matching top, five color overlay on green ground, h 13.7 cm (5³/₈ in.), glass, 18th–19th century, coll. Ina and Sandford Gadient

which, given the emperor's long reign, is not unreasonable. What has proven difficult is distinguishing between the wares made during this reign from those made afterwards. Thus far, it has been the custom to give Imperial attributions to glass vessels on the basis of their quality and marks. Present-day scholarship also takes into account their chemical composition. Quality is not a factor, the workmanship on some of the wares of dubious date is comparable to the finest, and not every piece of eighteenth century glass is of superlative quality. Given that glass materials from Boshan were used both by Imperial and Beijing craftsmen, it is clear that the chemical composition for some of these wares would be the same, making it difficult, if not impossible, to distinguish between them.

The use of 'western glass' presents another set of problems. In some cases the original object was ordered to be modified, and there is evidence to suggest that in other instances imported glass ingots were melted down and refashioned.[19] Since these ingots were compositionally similar to the potash-lead-silica glass in use in China, to identify glass as being unambiguously of, for instance, English or Chinese origin would be difficult on the basis of elemental composition alone.[20] If these wares met with Imperial approval, they, too, could have been inscribed with reign marks. Since neither area can provide a definitive answer, great caution should be taken when we view and assess these pieces.

10.15 Pair of covered jars, double overlay of green over pink on white, h 13 cm (5 in.), glass, 18th–19th century, Suntory Museum of Art, Tokyo

In all, the pieces discussed above, have presented us with an extraordinary inventory of glass for the Qianlong period. What we see in terms of color and form is: a wide range of shades, including the reddish-brown of aventurine glass; and a dozen forms ranging from tableware to the purely symbolic and decorative. The use of multi-color overlay decoration is suggested by references to 'five-color' glass, while other vessels were adorned with engraved floral designs or carved petal patterns. They attest to an unprecedented level of Chinese glassmaking, and to the fact that glass had found its own space among the arts.

NOTES

1. This was in accordance with the Chinese cyclical calendar. According to the Gregorian one, the dowager's empress sixtieth, seventieth, and eightieth birthdays fell on 11 January 1752, 20 December 1761, and 30 December 1771, respectively
2. Wan Yi (*c*.1998), pp. 247–8, 285
3. Erdai and Zhang Dingyou (1987). This work was originally completed in 36 *juan* in 1770
4. The presents are recorded in *juan* 18
5. Archives, no. 3437, Lam (2000), p. 55, contains a memorandum made in 1752 of 'Glass painted in oil colors with the hundred antiquities'
6. The chrysanthemum is the emblem of autumn, symbolizing a radiant middle age, and happy longevity
7. *Ruomu* = fabulous tree. It has leaves which shine at night
8. Wan Yi (*c*.1998), p. 27
9. Xu Song (1917), *juan* 2. This work also contains a record of the gifts for Xiaosheng's 60th and 70th birthdays
10. Zhang Weiyong (2000), p. 62, #8 & #9. The original lacquer chrysanthemum dish, still in the Imperial collection, is illustrated in Fig. 5
11. Archives, no. 3444, Lam (2000), p. 56
12. Shangdi is 'The Lord of the Heights'. His palace is at the highest point of the Nine Heavens situated in the Great Bear, *Beidou*. The emperor is Shangdi's son, hence 'Son of Heaven' *Tianzi*
13. The Purple Forbidden Cities, all of them from the beginning of China; the one in Beijing is only the most recent
14. The *ruyi* also evokes the *lingzhi* by its form. The *lingzhi*, when it grows, is an 'auspicious response' *rui ying* – heaven's own – to a ruler's enlightened government
15. He Chongyi and Zeng Zhaofeng (1995), pp. 11–19
16. Jiao Xiong, 'Changchun Yuan yuanlin jianzhu', *Yuanming Yuan*, vol. 3, pp. 12–24, and Zhang Enyin, 'Qing wudi yuzhi shiwen zhong de Yuanming Yuan shiliao', *Yuanming Yuan*, vol. 5, p. 156
17. See Lam (1993), pp. 33–6
18. *Mémoires concernant . . .* , vol. 2 (1777), pp. 477–9, 2 July 1775
19. Archives, nos 3405, 3443, and 3444, Lam (2000), pp. 52, and 56
20. Redknap and Freestone (1995), pp. 145–58

11

A Glassblowing Shop

Guangzhou (廣州 Canton), located at the southern tip of the empire, had been an historic center of trade since the Qin and Han periods. During the Qing dynasty, particularly after the ban on maritime trade with foreign countries was lifted in 1684, merchants came to purchase tea, silk, rhubarb, and a host of other articles. In return serge, rugs, enamels, incense, hardwood, clocks and glassware were imported. These exotic items permeated every sector of social life and induced a change in the handicrafts in Guangzhou. Traditional crafts such as embroidery, carpentry, metalwork, glassmaking, etc., all changed as artisans absorbed elements of foreign techniques and used them to develop an indigenous style of their own. The first generation of Chinese artists to work in oils and glass painting, watercolors, and copperplate engraving, emerged following the importation into Guangzhou of European examples of the same media. In order to explore this topic in some depth, it will be necessary to chart the course of this exchange from its beginnings.

Several ancient texts mention the firing of glass in Guangzhou. Additional references are found in Song dynasty texts, and the Ming period writer, Gao Lian's (高濂) opinion that imported glassware items were 'objects beneath the connoisseur', and 'not in good artistic taste', might indicate support for the local industry.[1] The Chinese of the Qing dynasty, however, greatly appreciated foreign glass and it is quite possible that Guangzhou glass artisans acquired the skills needed to make their own mirror and plate glass by observing the methods employed by French secular glassworkers. They had been brought to China in 1699, by the directors of the Compagnie de la Chine, with the intention of establishing a factory in Guangzhou.[2]

Tribute items of Guangzhou glassware were sent to Beijing on a fairly regular basis throughout the eighteenth century. The glass mirror with a floral border, the glass lantern, and a glass lantern with flowers mentioned in the *Suozi* 所子 list of the twenty-sixth day, eleventh month, sixty-first year of Kangxi (1722), were probably local products.[3] 'Snuff bottles of Guangzhou glass' were presented to Yongzheng in 1728,[4] and the thirteen glass bowls presented by Zu Binggui 祖秉圭, superintendent of the Guangdong maritime customs on the thirtieth day, fourth month, ninth year (1731) were also products of Guangzhou.[5] In 1756, the Maritime Customs Office (粵海關 *Yuehaiguan*) presented a glass-covered bowl, a glass dish, and a glass lens to the emperor. All of these were local products. Unfortunately, the cups were judged to be 'thin and brittle', and the emperor, it is reported, irritated with poor quality of the tribute, cancelled the standard reimbursement.[6]

The tribute from Guangdong province for 1771 included a pair of dressing mirrors in *zitan* frames, thought to be of Guangzhou or Suzhou manufacture, and four sheets of foreign glass length: 7 *chi* 5 *cun*, width: 4 *chi* 6 *cun*. The tribute from Guangdong and Guangxi for the seventh month, twentieth day, 1794, consisted of a pair of 'blessing and longevity' hanging screens, while that from Guangzhou in the twelfth month, fourth day consisted of a pair of hanging screens with glass hibiscus flowers, a pair of hanging screens with glass laurel flowers, a pair of hanging screens with glass antique objects, twelve pairs of square lanterns in glass and *zitan*, and twelve pairs of hexagonal lanterns in glass and *zitan*. All of these items are believed to have been made by Chinese artisans.[7]

The granting of licenses (1720) to a group of merchants to conduct trade with foreigners in the area, led to the establishment of a number of hongs. These served as the residences and trading headquarters for the western merchants. They were strictly confined to a small strip of land about a quarter of a mile long that ran along the Pearl river just outside the walls of the city. Countless books and diaries of the trade have chronicled the voyages to, and life in 'Canton', to which must be added those of the ubiquitous traveler. Hugh Gillan, physician attached to the Macartney embassy in 1793, wrote the following in regard to glass:

> The Canton artists, it is true, collect all the broken fragments of European glass they
> can find, which they pound and melt again in their furnaces; when melted they blow
> it into large globes or balloons [see Fig. 11.1] which they afterwards cut into pieces
> of various shapes and magnitudes as they want it. The chief use they make of it is for
> small looking glasses and toys. This is the only kind of glass they make . . . , and as
> they blow it extremely thin they find it easy to cut it with the steel chisels formerly
> mentioned; they do not seem to understand the manufacture of glass from the crude
> materials, nor to know exactly what they are.[8]

By the end of the eighteenth century another trend had developed: the production of Chinese paintings for the foreign trade. Watercolors and gouaches were avidly purchased by western merchants because of their convenient size and relatively low price. The watercolorists were in many instances the same painters who worked in oil on canvas. Many of the watercolors were done in sets, such as groups of port scenes, the trades, shop interiors, and Chinese scenes and landscapes. Those depicting craft and manufacturing processes varied in complexity of composition and detail, and the finest became some of the most desirable export watercolors painted.[9] A set of six pictures depicting Chinese artisans engaged in their trade *c*.1800, is typical of the earlier genre. Each is inscribed with Chinese

11.1 Interior of a glass-blowing shop, *China: A history of the laws, manners and customs of the people*, John Henry Gray, 1878, p. 233

characters describing the trade concerned, and in one of them a craftsman is depicted 'polishing glassware' (see Fig. 11.2).[10]

As in all fields, the most interesting items are the most unusual and unexpected ones. The Bibliothèque Nationale has two versions of the same subject – *Verre* (Oe 108, and Oe 109, 4⁰) – but the important one for identification bears a label from Youqua's studio.[11] Fashioned in the traditional manner, the label is an octagonal piece of white paper with a red outer border and the artist's name and address – 'Youqua Painter, Old street N° 34' – in red letters. Youqua painted pith paper albums in the 1850s. He was an extremely competent artist whose oeuvres encompassed port views, portraits, and still-life paintings of fruits and vegetables. Some of the examples which bear his label, lack the fine use of paint and attention to detail that one finds in Youqua's best works, and may have been painted by assistants working under his tutelage.

On closer examination, the designs in one of the sets in the Bibliothèque Nationale (Oe 108) have been filled in with colors, while the other set (Oe 109, 4⁰) was drawn only in ink. A description from another artist's studio provides an observation on the watercolorists and their methods: 'The design is usually limited to a mechanical tracing made very easy by the extreme transparency of the paper. Each artist has a collection of printed outlines and from them he chooses at will the elements of composition.'[12] After the outline was traced the colors were filled in. This technique was undoubtedly used here since the two sets under discussion are comprised of twelve identical designs, depicting the various stages employed to make plate glass.

11.2 Chinese Artist, *Polishing glassware*, 33.9 × 28.5 cm (13³/₄ × 11¹/₄ in.), watercolor, *c.*1800, photo courtesy Martyn Gregory Gallery, London

John Henry Gray's *Walks in the City of Canton* (Gray, 1975), contains a very detailed description of this of this process.

In the adjoining street of Wing-Hing-Tai-Kai 永興大街 we entered a glass blowing factory, which is styled Yan-Sunn, 仁信吹琉璃鋪, and where, of course, we had the pleasure of witnessing the process, which, in blowing glass, is, by the Cantonese, adopted. The ingredients, which, in the manufacture of glass, are, by the Cantonese employed, may be enumerated as follows: – Lead, sand, saltpetre, pewter, and broken pieces of flint glass[13] [see Fig. 11.3]. In the first instance, forty catties of pewter, and forty catties of lead, are

11.3 Youqua, *Weighing the raw glass materials*, 24.3 × 18.7 cm (9¹/₂ × 7¹/₄ in.), watercolor, *c.*1850, photographic reproduction by the Bibliothèque Nationale de France, Department Estampes, Res. Oe 108

11.4 Youqua, *Pouring the raw glass materials into the jars*, 24.3 × 18.7 cm (9¹/₂ × 7¹/₄ in.), *c.*1850, photographic reproduction by the Bibliothèque Nationale de France, Department Estampes, Res. Oe 108

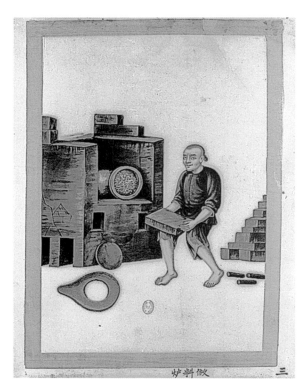

11.5 Youqua, *Placing the materials into the kiln*, 24.3 × 18.7 cm (9¹/₂ × 7¹/₄ in.), watercolor, *c.*1850, photographic reproduction by the Bibliothèque Nationale de France, Department Estampes, Res. Oe 108

11.6 Youqua, *Splitting the coal into small pieces*, 24.3 × 18.7 cm (9¹/₂ × 7¹/₄ in.), watercolor, *c.*1850, photographic reproduction by the Bibliothèque Nationale de France, Department Estampes, Res. Oe 108

cast into an iron pan, and, therein, together, well boiled. This mixture of lead and
pewter is a second time boiled, and, while boiling, is, at frequent intervals, well stirred
up. Moreover, to it, sixty catties of sand are added. This sand, or shek-fun, [sic]
as it is termed by the Cantonese, is brought from the district of Yin-tak, which
is one of the many political divisions into which the province of Kwang-tung
[廣東 Guangdong] is divided. The stones, from which this sand is obtained, abound
in the district, which we have just named. They are, ere they are brought to Canton,
reduced to a fine powder by being placed in mortars, and, then, beaten with pestles.
The pestles, for this purpose, are, by water wheels, kept in motion. This mixture of
lead, pewter, and fine sand, having been well boiled, is, then, poured into jars
[see Fig. 11.4], which are made either of mud, or clay. At the end of the ensuing
twenty-four hours, the ingredients in question [see Fig. 11.5], to which, sixty catties of
saltpetre, and a certain quantity of broken flint glass have been added, are again boiled.
This boiling process is continued throughout a period of twenty-four hours. The mixture,
now, being quite ready for the purposes of the glass blower, that workman takes an iron
blow pipe, and dips one end of it into the very midst of the caldron of boiling glass. He,
then, for the purpose of attaching to the end of this pipe, a portion of the thick boiling
mixture into which he has dipped it, turns it round, a few times [see Fig. 11.8]. On
removing the blow pipe from the caldron, it is found that to the end thereof, there is
attached as much of the thick boiling mixture, as would form a tennis ball. The blow
pipe, with this portion of glass still adhering to it, is, once more, dipped into the caldron
of boiling glass, and, with the view of gathering more of the mixture, is again turned
round in it. To the end of it, on its removal from the caldron, as much glass is attached,
as would form a large football. The upper end of the blow pipe is, now, applied to the
pipe of a large pair of Chinese bellows, which are suspended at a distance of seven or
eight feet, above the mouth of a pit, or excavation in the floor of the factory. The bellows
are approached by a ladder, and a man, having taken his station on the highest step
thereof, vigorously blows them in order that, by inflation, the ball of glass at the opposite
end of the blow pipe, may speedily assume the form and dimensions of a very large
globe. Thus the small ball of glass gradually swells out, and, at the same time, extends
itself to such a degree, as to reach into the pit to which, in a preceding sentence, commas
as per original text we have referred [see Fig. 11.9]. The large glass globe, thus formed, is,
in order that the blow pipe may be detached from it, placed, horizontally, on a cradle, or
stand which has been, previously, arranged to receive it [see Fig. 11.10]. The workman,
then, by means of a sharp knife, which he has previously immersed in cold water, makes
a circular mark, or incision around the neck of the glass globe, which is still very hot,
and, by gently striking the blow pipe with a hammer, succeeds in detaching it from the
brittle and transparent body, which, by its instrumentality, he has formed. Upon the
surface of the vast globe of glass, figures, such as squares, parallelograms, and circles,
are, by means of Chinese pens and ink, now drawn [see Fig. 11.11]. A workman, having
provided himself with a diamond, proceeds, in the next instance, to cut it [see Fig. 11.12],
into as many pieces as there are designs upon it. This labour, he very readily effects by

11.7 Youqua, *Placing the pieces of coal into the furnace*, 24.3 × 18.7 cm (9¹/₂ × 7¹/₄ in.), watercolor, *c*.1850, photographic reproduction by the Bibliothèque Nationale de France, Department Estampes, Res. Oe 108

11.8 Youqua, *Gathering the raw glass material in the form of a balloon*, 24.3 × 18.7 cm (9¹/₂ × 7¹/₄ in.), watercolor, *c*.1850, photographic reproduction by the Bibliothèque Nationale de France, Department Estampes, Res. Oe 108

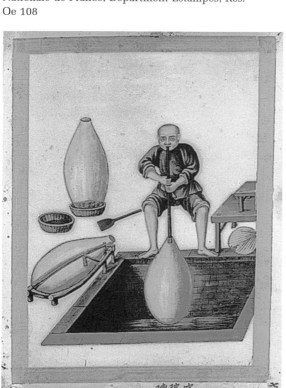

11.9 Youqua, *Blowing the glass balloon*, 24.3 × 18.7 cm (9¹/₂ × 7¹/₄ in.), watercolor, *c*.1850, photographic reproduction by the Bibliothèque Nationale de France, Department Estampes, Res. Oe 108

11.10 Youqua, *Cooling the glass balloon*, 24.3 × 18.7 cm (9¹/₂ × 7¹/₄ in.), watercolor, *c*.1850, photographic reproduction by the Bibliothèque Nationale de France, Department Estampes, Res. Oe 108

running his diamond along the various lines, which, by ink, have on the surface of the glass globe, been traced. Each of these pieces of glass, being an integral part of that which, previous to its mutilation, was a large glass globe, is of course, in the form of a crescent. To flatten each of them, therefore, is the duty, which next demands the attention of the workman. Now this duty, he readily discharges by arranging these various pieces of glass, that is four or six sheets at a time, on a flat smooth granite slab. This slab, with its brittle contents, he, then, places upon a pivot, which is steadfastly fixed in the centre of a hot charcoal furnace, or grate [see Fig. 11.13]. For a few seconds only, this slab is allowed to remain on the fire, and, while thereon, it is made to move in a circular form around the top of the pivot by which it is supported. On being removed from the fire, it is found that each piece of glass, which was placed upon it, is quite flat. These squares of glass are, eventually, sold either to looking glass makers, in order that they may be converted into mirrors, or to those artists, whose especial calling it is to paint pictures on glass, rather than on canvass, or paper.[14]

Gray's account is somewhat sparse with regard to the fuel used to heat the furnace. In one of the Bibliothèque Nationale's watercolors (see Fig. 11.6) a workman is shown splitting pieces of coal into small particles. Another watercolor (see Fig. 11.7) depicts a workman placing the pulverized coal into the furnace, and in the final one (see Fig. 11.14), plates of glass are in the process of being polished.

The Asian Export Art department at the Peabody-Essex Museum recently found a set of twelve works (AE 86334.25–32) on paper that show various scenes for the production of glass in China. The set is part of an album inscribed saying that it was purchased in 1847 by Admiral Preble. Before the advent of the camera, watercolors on pith paper were the only way travellers had of showing their families at home exactly where they had been, and what they had seen. Thus, as an accurate reflection of life in China, these albums played an extremely vital role in revealing Chinese culture to the West.

NOTES

1. Yang Boda (1991), p. 134
2. Pelliot (1929), pp. 252–67
3. Yang Boda (1987), pp. 40–41
4. Archives, no. 3313, Yang Boda (1983), p. 16, #24
5. Yang Boda (1987), p. 53
6. Archives, no. 3475, Yang Boda (1983), p. 16, #23
7. Yang Boda (1987), pp. 46–8
8. Gillan (1963), p. 299
9. Crossman (1973), pp. 92–118
10. *Trade Winds to China* (1987), pp. 10–13 no. 22b
11. Bibliothèque Nationale, Richelieu, Department des Estampes, Oe 108, and Oe 109, 4⁰
12. Crossman (1973), p. 120, #7
13. Gray's footnote explains, 'Large quantities of broken glass are forwarded to China, from Australia, for this purpose.'
14. Gray (1875), pp. 236–39

11.11 Youqua, *Tracing black lines in order to cut the sheets*, 24.3 × 18.7 cm (9¹/₂ × 7¹/₄ in.), watercolor, *c.*1850, photographic reproduction by the Bibliothèque Nationale de France, Department Estampes, Res. Oe 108

11.12 Youqua, *Cutting the glass into sheets*, 24.3 × 18.7 cm (9¹/₂ × 7¹/₄ in.), watercolor, *c.*1850, photographic reproduction by the Bibliothèque Nationale de France, Department Estampes, Res. Oe 108

11.13 Youqua, *Placing the glass sheets in the kiln*, 24.3 × 18.7 cm (9¹/₂ × 7¹/₄ in.), watercolor, *c.*1850, photographic reproduction by the Bibliothèque Nationale de France, Department Estampes, Res. Oe 108

11.14 Youqua, *Polishing the glass sheets*, 24.3 × 18.7 cm (9¹/₂ × 7¹/₄ in.), watercolor, *c.*1850, photographic reproduction by the Bibliothèque Nationale de France, Department Estampes, Res. Oe 108

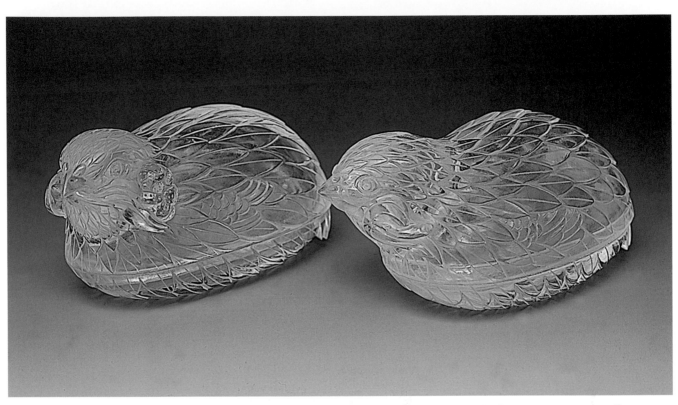

12.1 Pair of clear glass boxes and covers, shaped as quail, l 11 cm & 11.5 cm (4³/₈ in. & 4⁵/₈ in.), glass, *c.*1800, private coll.

12

Elegant Enjoyment: Scholar's Objects

We find in the nineteenth century that glass blowers were recruited from Boshan to work for the Jiaqing emperor 嘉慶 (r.1796–1820). A 1799 list of artisans active in the Imperial glassworks mentions that, in addition to these craftsmen, there were 'throwers', scrapers, 'filers', and *sula* 蘇拉 attendants. The throwers, scrapers, and filers all worked with traditional lapidary tools to finish the glass vessels. *Sula*-were general workmen or apprentices, who did whatever else was required. Recorded and identified are Boshan artisans, Hao Zhen 郝珍 and Hao Lan 郝藍, who worked in the service of the emperor from the seventeenth to the twenty-second years (1812–17) of the reign. Still another brother, Hao Hai 郝海 is listed for 1817.[1] The Imperial workshop maintained the general standard of Qianlong glass, and made many carefully crafted pieces for use in the New Year and birthday festivities. This custom can be traced back to the second year of Yongzheng's reign (1724) when, in order to curry favor with the emperor, Prince Yi instructed all the workshops that, henceforth, they were to produce some small handicraft work in time for the *Duanwujie* 端午節 (Dragon Boat Festival), *Wanshoujie* 萬壽節 (Emperor's birthday), and *Nianjie* 年節 (New Year Festival).[2]

Neither Yongzheng nor his successor Qianlong had set strict quotas on the number of annual pieces to be made. However, when Jiaqing ascended the throne, he ordered that 301 pieces of glass must be made each year. The artisans had to present eighty-one plates, cups, small circular dishes, and sixty snuff bottles in time for the Dragon Boat (*Duanwujie*) Festival, and 100 plates, cups, and circular dishes, and sixty bottles at the New Year. In the twenty-fifth year of Jiaqing (1820), the offering was reduced to 106 glass objects.[3]

In 1814, Jiaqing asked Yongxing 永瑆, the first Prince Cheng,[4] who excelled in calligraphy, to select the best specimens of his handwriting. The emperor had them inscribed on stone and reproduced in the form of rubbings, and named the collection *Yijin Zhai fatie* 詒晉齋法帖, after the studio where Yongxing stored a large collection of books and objects d'art. The studio had been named after a famous album leaf of calligraphy, known as the *Pingfu tie* 平復帖, which the prince had received as a 'bequest' from his grandmother, Empress Dowager Xiaosheng. This hallmark, *Yijin Zhai* 詒晉齋 (The Jin Bequest Studio), can be

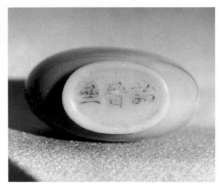

12.2 Snuff bottle, greenish turquoise, base incised: *Yijin Zhai*, h 5.08 cm (2 in.), glass, 1770–1823 private coll.

12.3 Base mark, 12.2

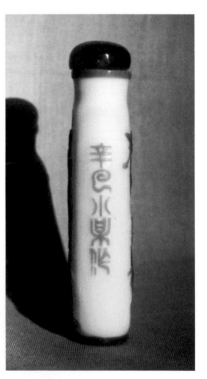

12.4 Wang Su, snuff bottle, rose pink over white, h 6.01 cm (2³/₈ in.), glass, 1821, private coll.

12.5 Side 12.4, inscription: *1821, made by Xiaomei*

found in various styles on Yongxing's seals, ancient paintings, calligraphy, and snuff bottles[5] such as the greenish-turquoise glass on shown in Fig. 12.2, where the last character *zhai* ('studio'), was rendered in its most reduced form (see Fig. 12.3).[6]

At this time, glassmaking in Beijing did not include the initial process of glass melting, but was solely a fabrication of objects from glass ingots known as *liao qi* 料器, implying 'glass made with Shandong (Boshan) *liao*.' This practice seems to apply also to a very distinctive group of wares commonly identified by the term 'Yangzhou School.' At present, there is no evidence to indicate the existence of glassmaking in Yangzhou, with the closest site being Suzhou. However, the history of manufacture there is obscure, and according to Liang Tongshu 梁同書, during the Qing dynasty the quality of 'su-made' glass was extremely poor.[7] Therefore the use of the term Yangzhou may be viewed as indicating the source of the finished product, and not the site of all stages of its production.

A number of independent artists from various areas of China had settled in Yangzhou where they became known as the 'Eccentric Painters of Yangzhou'. Gerard Tsang has traced the development of the Yangzhou glass bottles to this style of painting. Wang Su's (王素) art name, Xiaomei 小梅, came to his attention while he was preparing an exhibition of fan paintings for the Hong Hong Museum of Art. Tsang realized that Wang's signatures and seals were similar to those found on 'seal school' snuff bottles. Intrigued, he researched further and found an entry for Wang Su in the *Biographies of Seal Carvers*,[8] which indicated that, in addition to being a painter, Wang Su was also a seal carver, who was capable of working with glass. This certainly seems to be the case from a small group of bottles signed by Wang Su with the character *zuo* 作 ('made by', see Figs. 12.4 and 12.5).

One of the few objects from this school, other than snuff bottles, is an important vase from the Firestone collection (see Fig. 12.6).[9] The overlay color of a subtle rose pink is carved in a manner reminiscent of the 'Eccentrics' style of painting. An inscription on the neck reads 'made by Master Li' with a cyclical date to the *dingchou* 丁丑 year (1817), while a seal on the base reads Weizhi zhenwan 維之珍玩 (For the precious enjoyment of Weizhi). Weizhi is thought to be one of Li Junting's (李均亭) art names, another being simply Junting. From other inscriptions where Li refers to himself as 'Mr. Li of Jingjiang', we surmise that he came from Jingjiang – which is the ancient namefor Zhenjiang, a town some twenty miles from Yangzhou (see Fig. 12.7).

Another noteable example, with a link to Imperial ownership, is a multiple overlay glass snuff bottle which has a three character *Shende Tang* 李均亭 (Hall of Prudent Virtue) mark, inscribed on its base (see Figs. 12.9 and 12.10). The Shende Tang was the residential palace of the Daoguang emperor 道光 (*r*.1821–50), at the western side of the *Jiuzhou Qingyan* 九洲清晏 (Hall of Peace in the Nine Continents), in the Yuanming Yuan (see Fig. 12.8). Porcelain ware bearing this mark were specially commissioned by the emperor for his use there,[10] and five other

12.6 Li Junting, vase, rose pink over white, h 17.2 cm (6³/₄ in.), glass, 1817, coll. Firestone, Christie's, NY, 22 March 1991, #504

12.7 Li Junting, snuff bottle, white over medium blue, h 6.2 cm (2¹/₂ in.), glass, 1819, coll. Mary and George Bloch

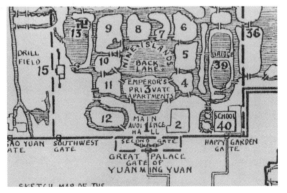

12.8 Diagram with detail of the emperor's residential quarters in the Yuanming Yuan

12.9 Snuff bottle, carved double overlay of green on pink on white, base incised *Shende Tang*, 6.9 cm (2³/₄ in.) glass, 1831–50, coll. J. Grimberg

12.10 Base mark, 12.9

12.11 Jar, light red, with four rams carved in relief, base incised *Xingyouheng Tang*, h 9 cm (4¹/₈ in.), glass, 1836–54, coll. Simon Kwan

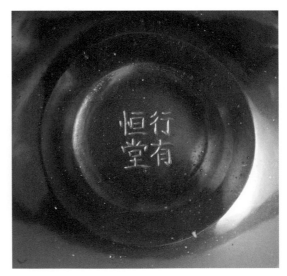

12.12 Base mark, 12.11

pieces – three paintings and two glass snuff bottles – are known also to bear the *Shende Tang* mark in some form.

The quality of the glass in the Daoguang era was considered to be below previous standards, and some of the reign marks were executed carelessly. During the reign of Xianfeng 咸豐 (1851–61) the quality of the glass improved. It has been said that time-consuming objects, such as carved glass finished by gem-cutting techniques, were no longer produced, and that their disappearance might be closely tied to Xianfeng's imperial edict which stated: 'All objects should be simple and all inscriptions legible.'[11] Very few pieces bear this reign mark.[12]

Zaiquan 載銓, the fifth Prince Ding, was known to have been a great patron of all kinds of handicrafts in Beijing, and a keen collector. His hall mark, *Xingyouheng Tang* 行有恆堂 (Hall of Perseverance), can be found on works of art ranging from snuff bottles, molded gourds, ceramics, glass, jade and hard stone carvings. The hall, itself, was located in Prince Ding's garden, the Weixiu Yuan 蔚秀園 (Garden of Luxuriant Elegance), which was to the north of the Changchun Yuan section of the Yuanming Yuan.[13] Among the glass objects bearing the *Xingyouheng Tang* mark is a light red glass jar with four rams carved in relief around its neck (see Figs. 12.11 and 12.12). A water pot of striated blue-green glass set with two *chilong* and cloud scrolls (see Fig. 12.13), provides a rare example in overlay glass. It bears an incised seal script mark (see Fig. 12.14).

With the confiscation of all missionary property in 1827, and the destruction of the Yuanming Yuan in 1860, glassmaking ceased at both Imperial workshops. Oddly enough, the building which housed the original glass workshop (*bolichang*) on Canchikou, remained, and when D. F. Rennie M.D. was in Beijing (1861), he related that he was shown 'a building and grounds where in former years the Jesuits manufactured glass, and which formed a portion of their property. Since the resettlement of the Mission at Peking, the priests applied to have this restored, but the reply they got from the Government was to the effect that it had been given to their predecessors to manufacture glass for the Emperor; and that if they would undertake to do the same, they might have it back, but not otherwise.'[14] Rather surprisingly, in 1864 the missionaries received the deed for the terrain from the Chinese government, but there is no evidence to suggest that they ever re-established a glass workshop. This leaves us with the thorny problem as to the place of manufacture for subsequent Imperial, reign-marked glassware.

A period of relative stability (post 1864), during Tongzhi's reign 同治, (1862–74), promoted Beijing's local glass industry, and local craftsmen sent objects to the Qing court every year. Boshan was still one of China's most important glassmaking centers (see Fig. 12.15). When the Rev. Alexander Williamson visited this site in 1869, he found the artisans engaged in:

> making excellent window-glass, blowing bottles of various sizes, moulding cups of every
> description, and making lanterns, beads and ornaments in endless variety. They also run

12.14 Base mark, 12.13

12.13 Water pot swirled blue-green, with carved overlay, base incised *Xingyouheng Tang*, h 5.4 cm (2¹/₈ in.), glass, 1836–54, coll. Robert L. Chasin

12.15 Old town area of Boshan by the Shaolu river, *Schantung und Deutsch = China*, Leipzig, 1898

12.16 Recumbent animal figures of horse and water-buffalo, black, l 20.5–23 cm (8–10 in.), glass, 19th century, coll. Ina and Sandford Gadient

it into rods, about thirty inches long, which they tie up in bundles, and export to all parts of the country ... The glass is extremely pure, they colour it most beautifully, and have attained considerable dexterity in manipulation; many of the articles are finely finished.[15]

The imitation of jade and hardstones became a feature of later Chinese glass. A horse and an ox replicate in glass an important theme in jade carving, where the two animals are often paired (see Fig. 12.16). Gratitude for the contributions of these two animals to traditional agricultural society manifests itself in the form of temple deities.[16] Horse-breeders worshiped the image of the Horse King 馬王 (also known as the Horse General 馬將軍), who was usually accompanied by a similar figure for the Ox King 牛王 (or general). The former had by his side a small model of a horse, and the latter that of an ox.[17] These images played an important part in folk belief which held that they would protect property and insure a good harvest.

Hardstone imitations include a scholar's glass brush holder (*bitong* 筆筒), which simulates malachite. The *bitong* is superbly carved with a longevity theme of a *shouxing* 壽星 (the star of old age, portrayed as an elderly man; a person on his birthday) seated against a cavernous grotto and rocks (see Fig. 12.17), the inscribed reverse bears a date for the autumn month of 1834 (see Fig. 12.18), and the base has a Daoguang reign mark within a double square (see Fig. 12.19). Such

117

12.17 Brush holder (*bitong*), with high relief carving of longevity theme, base incised *Daoguang nianzhi*, h 14.6 cm (5³/₄ in.), glass simulating malachite, 1834, private coll., Hong Kong

12.19 Daoguang reign mark (1821–51), base 12.17

12.18 Reverse of 12.17, with seal script inscription

12.20 Mallet shaped vase, green over snowflake, h 19.05 cm (7¹/₂ in.), glass, 1850–1900, coll. Alan E. Feen

objects were intended for the scholar's desk and seem to reflect a taste distinct from that of the Imperial court.

An overlay glass vase (see Fig. 12.20), attributed to the second half of the nineteenth century, would seem to have been designed to evoke the vaule of quiet contemplation. It depicts Lu Yu 陸羽, the author of the *Chaqing* 茶經, a famous Tang dynasty work describing the origin and preparation of tea. In this rendition Lu Yu is seated on a straw mat inside a rocky formation holding a fan while being served by two attendants. Some of the characters just above the scene refer to the sage and 'making tea by the Jade river' (玉川料茶, *yuchuan liaocha*). One of the oval seals reads *Nan Xiang* 南翔: 'Flying towards the south', which may be a name, either of the craftsman who made this piece, or the person for whom it was made.

Lin Youlin's (林有麟) *Suyuan shihpu* 素園石譜, contains illustrations of the rocks purported to have been collected by the Song emperor Huizong 徽宗 (*r.*1101–25). The Chinese have always loved rocks with natural holes in them; they admired them for their shape, their texture and their feel, and respected them as though they were actual living things. Known collectively as *guaishi* 怪石 ('strange stones'), these rocks were often treated like sculpture, to be placed on a scholar's desk for his elegant enjoyment while he wrote or painted. They were always regarded by the scholar class in the context of their literary and symbolic associations, and various attempts to express, or at least suggest, some of these ideas in glass may have prompted the production of some of the most esoteric objects in that medium (see Fig. 12.21).

Towards the end of the century, the Qing ruling class took a series of steps designed to monopolize the nation's glassmaking industry. They established strict rules to prevent Beijing merchants from buying and using glass ingots from Boshan, and established state-run glass companies. These restrictions caused a severe depression to Boshan's economy, until the government relented and established a glass company (1902) at Liukeng, a town northwest of Boshan. After the fall of the Qing dynasty in 1912, the local people set up their own glass factory and made flat plate glass. Even so, during the ensuing turbulent years, artisans were hard pressed to make a living, and Beijing and Boshan glassmakers survived by concentrating their efforts into making various colored wares. Some of these were in imitation of Imperial pieces.

In 1993, the Liuli Gongfang 琉璃工房 held a small showing of glass works at the Palace Museum in Beijing, which later accepted one statue – a Buddha seated under a large hand – into its permanent collection. The founder of this enterprise, Loretta (Hui-shan) Yang 楊惠姍, had given up her career as Taiwan's leading film actress, to devote herself, instead, to the creation of modern Chinese glass. She studied and mastered the unique technique of *patê-de-verre*, called in Chinese *shuijing tuola jingtao* 水晶脫蠟精鑄, casting. This technique is similar to the *cire-perdue* (lost wax) technique used in bronze casting during the Spring and Autumn period (770–476 BC), a connection which led Yang Boda to describe

12.21 Vase, amber over white, base incised *Guangxu nianzhi*, h 19.8 cm (7³/₄ in.), glass, 1875–1908; scholar's rock, coral-orange, h 10.16 cm (4 in.), glass, *c.*1900, coll. William Lillyman, photograph by Ognan Borissov

Loretta Yang as 'the true inheritor of a profoundly unremarked history that goes back to the traditional sources of the nation, like some form of historical inevitability' (see Fig. 12.22).[18]

Loretta Yang is one of a tiny handful working to promote modern Chinese glass art. By using their acute powers of observation to create sculptured works in glass which are imbued with a traditional Chinese artistic vocabulary and human philosophy, these modern glass artisans are creating magnificent pieces that constitute a new milestone on the Chinese 'Glass Road'.

NOTES

1. Lam (2000), pp. 42, 43, and Yang Boda (1983), p. 13
2. Xia Gengqi (1995), p. 18
3. Yang Boda (1991), p. 146
4. For a biography of Yongxing see Hummel (ed.) (1943), pp. 962–3
5. Wang Shixiang (1985), pp. 193–5
6. For an example with the mark in seal script see *Snuff Bottles of the Ch'ing Dynasty*, Hong Kong Museum of Art, presented by the Urban Council in Association with the International Chinese Snuff Bottle Society, 1978, p. 73, #81
7. Yang Boda (1991), p. 137
8. Tsang (1979), pp. 5–10
9. Christie's, New York, 22 March 1991, #54
10. Lam (1993), #19
11. Yang Boda (1991), p. 148.
12. For an example of a marked snuff bottle see Xia Genqi (1995), p. 179, #53.
13. Lam (1993), #23, and Hummel (ed.) (1943), pp. 728–9
14. Rennie (1865), vol. 2, p. 99
15. Williamson (1870), vol. 1, pp. 131–2
16. Jian Rong-zong (2002), pp. 20–31
17. Williams (1973), pp. 191–2
18. Yang Boda (1998)

12.22 Loretta Yang, *Buddha Omnipresent*, h 23 cm (9 in.), glass, 2000, photograph courtesy of Liuligongfang

Bibliography

Manuscript Materials
Paris
Archives Congregation de la Mission, Paris
Archives des Affaires Étrangères, Paris
Archives des Missions Étrangères, Paris
Archives jésuites de la province de Paris, Vanves

Rome
Archivum Generale Ordinis Fratrum Minorum
Archivum S. Congregationis de Propaganda Fide
Archivum Romanum Societatis Iesu

Vatican City
Archivio Segreto Vaticano
Bibliotheca Apostolica Vaticana

Printed Works
Arnold, Lauren (1999), *Princely Gifts and Papal Treasures: The Franciscan Mission to China and its Influence on the Art of the West 1250–1350*, San Francisco: Desiderata Press.
Berger, Patricia (1997), 'Vanity of Vanities: Adorning the Body in Life and in Death', *Orientations*, March, vol. 29, p. 67.
Brill, Robert, (1963) 'Ancient Glass', *Scientific American*, November, pp. 120–31.
Brill, Robert (1968), 'The scientific investigation of ancient glasses', *Proceedings: Eighth International Congress on Glass*, Brussels, pp. 47–68.
Brill, Robert H. (1975), 'Crizzling – A Problem in Glass Conservation', *Conservation in Archaeology and the Applied Arts*, International Institute for Conservation.
Brill, Robert H. and Martin, John H. (eds) (1991), *Scientific Research in Early Chinese Glass*, Corning, NY: The Corning Museum of Glass.
Cammann, Schuyler V. R. (1962), *Substance and Symbol in Chinese Toggles*, Philadelphia: University of Pennsylvania Press.
Cammann, Schuyler V. R. (1982), 'Animal Subjects', *Miniature Art from Old China*, exh. cat. Montclair Art Museum, Montclair New Jersey, pp. 16–18.
Chang Lin-sheng (1987), 'Qing Enameled Glass' *Chinese Glass of the Qing Dynasty, 1644–1911: The Robert H. Clague Collection*, Claudia Brown and Donald Rabiner (eds), Phoenix, AZ: Phoenix Art Museum, pp. 87–93.

Chang Lin-sheng (1991a), 'Ch'ing Dynasty Painted Enamelled Glassware', *Arts of Asia*, **21** (3), May–June, pp. 95–107.
Chang Lin-sheng (1991b), *Snuff Bottles in the Collection of the National Palace Museum*, Taipei: National Palace Museum, pp. 25–49.
Chang Li-tuan (1997), *Kung-Ting Chih Ya: Ch'ing-Tai Fang-ku Che Hua-yi Yu-chih T'e-Chih T'u-lu* (The Refined Taste of the Emperor: Special Exhibition of Archaic and Pictorial Jades of the Ch'ing Court), exh. cat. Taipei: National Palace Museum, pp. 51–2, 189–209, #24.
Crossman, Carl L. (1973), *The China Trade: Exports Paintings, Furniture, Silver and Other Objects*, Princeton: The Pyne Press.
Curtis, Emily Byrne (1993a), 'Chinese Glass and the Vatican Records', *Transactions of the Oriental Ceramic Society*, London: The Oriental Ceramic Society, **57**, pp. 50–8.
Curtis, Emily Byrne (1993b), 'European Contributions to the Chinese Glass of the Early Qing Period', *Journal of Glass Studies*, Corning, NY: The Corning Museum of Glass, **35**, pp. 91–101.
Curtis, Emily Byrne (1998), 'Chinese Glassmaking: Tradition and Transformation', *Arts of Asia*, **26** (6) November–December, pp. 98–107.
Curtis, Emily Byrne (1999), 'Foucquet's List: Translation and Comments on the Color "Blue Sky After Rain"', *Journal of Glass Studies*, Corning, NY: The Corning Museum of Glass, **41**, pp. 147–52.
Curtis, Emily Byrne (2001), 'Plan of the Emperor's Glassworks', *Arts Asiatiques*, Annales du musée national des Arts asiatiques-Guimet et du musée Cernuschi, **56**, pp. 81–90.
Curtis, Emily Byrne and Ricardo Joppert (2001), 'Myriad Years and Abundant Blessings: Auspicious Gifts for Empress Xiaosheng', *Oriental Art Magazine*, XLVII (1), pp. 2–9.
Curtis, Emily Byrne (2003), 'Qingzhao di boli zhizao yuye suhui shihzai Canchikou di zuofang' ('Qing Dynasty Glass Making and the Jesuit Workshop at Canchikou'), *Gugong bowuyuan yuankan*, **1**, pp. 62–71, Chinese translation by Mi Chenfeng.
Daxue, trans. J. Legge, *Great Learning*, Dover, New York, 1971.

Dehergne, Joseph (1973), *Répertoire des Jésuites de Chine de 1552 à 1800*, Rome: Institutum Historicum S. I.

D'Incarville, Pierre (1812), 'Catalogue alphabétique des plantes et autres objets d'histoire naturelle en usage en Chine', *Mémoires de la Société Imperiale des Naturalistes de Moscou*, Moscow, **3**, pp. 103–28, **4**, pp. 26–87.

Erdai, E. and Zhang Dingyou, comp. (1987), *Guochao gongshi*, Publisher's note; reprint of 1925 edition, Beijing: Beijing guji zhuban she.

Favier, Alphonse (1897), *Péking: Histoire et Description*, Imprimerie Lazaristes au Pé-T'ang Beijing.

Gao Shiqi (1912–13), 'Pengshan miji' in *Guxue huikan*, Tengshi, comp. Shanghai, **2**.

Gillan, Hugh (1963), 'Observations of the State of Medicine, Surgery, and Chemistry in China' in *An Embassy to China*, Hamden, CT: Archon Books, Hamden.

Gongzhongdang Kangxichao zouzhe (Secret Palace Memorials of the Kangxi Period) (1976), Taipei: National Palace Museum, vol. 6.

Gray, John Henry (1875), *Walks in the City of Canton*, Hong Kong: De Souza & Co, Victoria.

Guilbaud, Pauline (1998), *Archives des Lazaristes de Pékin: Inventaire*, Nantes: Centre des Archives Diplomatiques de Nantes.

Guo Xiang (1998), *Nanhua zhen jing zhu shu/ Guo Xiang shu*, Beijing Shi: Zhonghua shu ju.

Hao Yulin (1731), *Guangdong Tongzhi*, [Beijing (?)].

Hardie, Peter (1990), 'Glass in China: Late Ming to Early Qing', *Transactions of the Oriental Ceramic Society*, London: The Oriental Ceramic Society, **55**, pp. 9–28.

Hardie, Peter (1996), 'Glass in China: Questions and Some Answers', *Vormen uit Vuur*, Leiden, **58**, (2), pp. 2–14.

He Chongyi and Zeng Zhaofeng (1995), *Yuanming Yuan yuanlin yishu*, Beijing: Kexue chu banshe.

Honey, W. B. (1937), 'Early Chinese Glass', *Burlington Magazine*, LXXI, (CDXVI), Nov., pp. 211–23.

Hummel, Arthur W. (ed.) (1943), *Eminent Chinese of the Ch'ing Period 1644–1912*, Washington, D.C.: Government Printing Office.

Jian Rong-zong (2002), 'Equine Culture in the Year of the Horse', *Art of the Zodiac*, exh. cat. The Chinese Information and Cultural Center, New York, pp. 20–31.

Kleiner, Robert (1995), *Chinese Snuff Bottles in the Mary & George Bloch Collection*, The British Museum.

Kwan, Simon (2001), *Early Chinese Glass*, Hong Kong: Art Museum, The Chinese University of Hong Kong.

Lam, Peter Y. K. (ed.) (1993), *Elegant Vessels for the Lofty Pavilion: The Zande Lou Gift of Porcelain with Studio Marks*, Hong Kong: Art Museum, The Chinese University of Hong Kong.

Lam, Peter Y. K. (2000), 'The Glasshouse of the Qing Imperial Household Department', *Elegance and Radiance: Grandeur in Qing Glass, The Andrew K. F. Lee Collection*, Peter Y. K. Lam and Humphry K. R. Hui (eds), Hong Kong: Art Museum, The Chinese University of Hong Kong.

Lane, Arthur (1974), *Early Islamic Pottery: Mesopotamia, Egypt and Persia*, London: Faber & Faber.

Lawson, Jessica (1997), 'The Reuse of Ancient Jades', *Colloquies on Art & Archaeology in Asia*, no. 18, Percival David Foundation of Chinese Art, London: University of London, p. 179.

Lettres édifiantes et curieuses, écrits des missions étrangères, (1717–76), Paris: N. Le Clerc, vols. 1–34.

Little, Stephen *et al.* (2000), *Taoism and the Arts of China*, Chicago: Art Institute of Chicago, pp. 28, 227.

Liu An (ed.) (1875), *Huainanzi*, Zi Shu Bo Jia ('Books by the Thinkers from the Hundred Schools'), Hubie, Chongwen Press.

Loehr, George (1963), 'Missionary Artists of the Manchu Court', *Transactions of the Oriental Ceramic Society*, London: **34**, pp. 51–67.

Maitre, Henri Bernard, S. J. (1949), 'Un correspondant de Bernard de Jussieu en Chine. Le Pere Le Chéron d'Incarville', *Archives internationales d'Histoire des Sciences*, Cathasia: **II**, pp. 1–58.

Mehlman, Felice (1983), *Phaidon Guide to Glass*, Englewood Cliffs, NJ.

Mémoires concernant l'histoire, les sciences, les arts, les usages, etc. des Chinois par les Missionnaires de Pékin (1777–91), Paris: Nyon, vols 1–15.

Michaelson, Carol (2000), 'The Use of Archaism as Decorative Motif in Snuff Bottles', *Journal of the International Chinese Snuff Bottle Society*, XXXIII, 3, pp. 4–7.

Moore, Oliver (1998), 'Islamic glass at Buddhist sites in medieval China' *Gilded and Enamelled Glass from the Middle East*, Rachel Ward (ed.), London: British Museum Press, pp. 78–84.

Morache, G. (1869), *Pékin et ses habitants*, Paris: J.-B. Baillière et Fils.

Moss, Hugh (2001), 'Chronological List: Primary Sources' in *A Treasury of Chinese Snuff Bottles. The Mary and George Bloch Collection, vol. 5, Glass*, Hong Kong: Herald International Ltd., pp. 56–90.

National Palace Museum (1995), *Chin-t'ung Fo-chiao Kung-chu Te-chan* (A Special Exhibition of Buddhist Gilt Votive Objects), #7, #9, #10, #19, and #21.

Pelliot, Paul (1929), 'L'Origine des relations de la France avec la Chine: Le Premier Voyage de l'Amphritrite en Chine', *Journal des Savants*, Paris, June, pp. 252–67.

Pfister, Louis, S. J. (1932), *Notices Biographiques et Bibliographiques sur Les Jésuites de L'Ancienne Mission de Chine 1552–1773*, Shanghai, 2 vols, Reprinted by Chinese Materials Center, Inc., San Francisco, CA, 1976.

Plesch, Peter H. (1980), 'Some Decorative Techniques Found in Later Chinese Glass', *Transactions of the Oriental Ceramic Society*, The Oriental Ceramic Society, **44**, pp. 47–66.

Redknap, Mark and Freestone, Ian C. (1995), 'Eighteenth-Century Glass Ingots From England:

Bibliography

Further Light on the Post-Medieval Glass Trade',
*Occasional Paper 109, Department of Scientific
Research*, London: British Museum, pp. 145–58.

Reil, Sebald (1978), *Kilian Stumpf 1655–1720:
Ein Würzburger Jesuit am Kaiserhof zu Peking*,
Munster, West Germany: Aschendorff.

Rennie, D. F. (1865), *Peking and the Pekingese*,
London: John Murray.

Robins, Dan (2001), review of Paul Rakita Goldin,
'Rituals of the Way: The Philosophy of Xunzi',
The Journal of Asian Studies, **6**, no. 4, p. 1153.

Rogers, J. M. (1998), 'European Inventories as a
source for the distribution of Mamluk enamelled
glass' in *Gilded and Enamelled Glass from the
Middle East*, Rachel Ward (ed.), London: British
Museum Press, pp. 69–77.

Rosenzweig, Daphne Lange (1991), *The Fine Arts
Group Collection of Later Chinese Paintings*,
Jerusalem: Levy Publishers, in association with
the Museum of Fine Arts, St. Petersburg,
FL, #17.

Rosso, Antonio Sisto (1948), *Apostolic Delegations
to China of the Eighteenth Century*, South
Pasadena, CA: P. D. and Ione Perkins.

Shan Guoqiang *et al.* (1990), *The Forbidden
City: Court Culture of the Chinese Emperors
(1644–1911)*, Rotterdam: Museum Boymans-van
Beuningen, p. 76.

Shi Meiguang and Zhou Fuzheng (1993), 'Some
Chinese Glasses of the Qing Dynasty', *Journal
of Glass Studies*, Corning, NY: The Corning
Museum of Glass, Corning, N.Y., **35**, pp. 102–105.

Soulié de Morant, Georges (1916), *L'Epopée des
Jesuits Français en Chine, 1534–1928*, Paris:
B. Grasset.

Tian Jiaqing (1993), 'Early Qing Furniture in a Set
of Qing Court Paintings', *Orientations*, **24** (1),
pp. 32–40.

*Trade Winds to China: An Exhibition of Early
Pictures relating to the Far East* (1987), Martyn
Gregory Catalogue 47, London, summer,
pp. 10–13, no. 22b.

Tsang, Gerard C. C. (1979), 'Yangchou Seal Bottles',
*Journal of The International Chinese Snuff
Society*, vol. XI, no. 2, pp. 5–10.

Verdier, P. le (1904), 'Documents Historiques:
Quelques Lettres du P. D'Incarville, Missionnaire
en Chine', *Bulletins de La Société de L'Histoire de
Normandie*, Paris, **9**, pp. 73–9.

Wan Yi, chief comp. (c.1998), *Daily Life in the
Forbidden City* (*Qingdai gongding shenghuo*),
New York, NY: Viking.

Wang Shixiang (1985), 'Xijin Lu Ji Pingfu tie
liuchuan kaolue', *Gugong bowuyuan canbao lu*,
Hong Kong, pp. 193–5.

Wang Shizhen (1705), *Xiangzu biji zixu*,
[Beijing (?)].

Watson, James C. and Rawski, Evelyn S. (eds)
(1988), *Death Ritual in Late Imperial* and *Modern
China*, Berkeley: University of California Press,
chapter one, p. 3.

White, Helen (1992), 'Introduction' in *Snuff Bottles
from China: The Victoria and Albert Museum
Collection*, London: Bamboo Publishing Ltd.

Whitefield, Roderick (1982–3), *The Art of
Central Asia: The Stein Collection in the British
Museum*, Tokyo: Kodansha International, vol. 2,
Fig. 20.

Williams, C. A. S. (1973), *Outlines of Chinese
Symbolism*, repr. Ch'eng Wen Publishing
Company, Taipei, pp. 191–2.

Williamson, Alexander (1870), *Journeys in North
China, Manchuria, and Eastern Mongolia*,
London: Smith, Elder & Co.

Witek, John, W., S. J. (1982), *Controversial Ideas
in China and in Europe: A Biography of
Jean-François Foucquet, S. J. (1665–1741)*,
Rome: Institutum Historicum S. I.

Witek, John W., S. J. (1999), 'Sent to Lisbon, Paris
and Rome: Jesuit Envoys of the Kangxi Emperor',
*Instituto Universitario Orientale, Collana 'Matteo
Ripa'*, Napoli, no. XVI, pp. 336–7.

Wu Changyuan (1778), *Chenyuan shilueh*,
[Beijing (?)].

Xia Gengqi (1995), 'A Brief Introduction of the Qing
Court Snuff Bottles' in *Masterpieces of Snuff
Bottles in the Palace Museum*, Beijing:
The Forbidden City Publishing House of the
Palace Museum, pp. 1–38.

Xu Song, comp. (1917), 'Dongchao chongyang lu'
in *Songlin congshu jiabian*, [China].

Yang Boda (1983), 'Qing dai boli gaishu' ('A brief
account of glass of the Qing dynasty'), *Gugong
bowuyuan yuankan*, **4**, pp. 3–16.

Yang Boda (1984), 'Yuan Ming Qing gongxi meishu
zongxu' ('A summary of arts and crafts of the
Yuan, Ming and Qing Dynasties'), *Gugong
bowuyuan yuankan*, **4**, pp. 3–14.

Yang Boda (1987), 'The Characteristics and
Status of Guangdong Handicrafts as seen from
Eighteenth-Century Tributes from Guangdong the
Collection of the Former Qing Palace', *Tributes
from Guangdong to the Qing Court*, Hong Kong:
Art Gallery, jointly presented by The Palace
Museum, Beijing & The Art Gallery, The Chinese
University of Hong Kong, pp. 39–67.

Yang Boda (1991), 'An Account of Qing Dynasty
Glassmaking', *Scientific Research in Early Chinese
Glass*, Robert H. Brill and John H. Martin (eds),
Corning, NY: The Corning Museum of Glass,
pp. 131–50.

Yang Boda (1998), 'A New Milestone Along the
Chinese "Glass Road"', *Liuligongfang: Exhibition
of the Loretta Hui-shan Yang Chinese Glass Art
Creative Studio*, Beijing: Palace Museum.

Yeh, Catherine Vance (1998), 'Reinventing Ritual:
Late Qing Handbooks for Proper Customer
Behavior in Shanghai Courtesan Houses',
Late Imperial China, **19**, no. 2, pp. 43, 49.

Yi Jialiang and Tu Shujin (1991), 'Chinese
Glass Technology in Boshan Around the 14th
Century', *Scientific Research in Early Chinese
Glass*, Robert H. Brill and John H. Martin (eds),
Corning, NY: The Corning Museum of Glass,
pp. 99–102.

Yu Chunfang (1994), 'Guanyin: The Chinese
Transformation of Avalokitêshvara' in *Latter Days
of the Law: Images of Chinese Buddhism 850–
1850*, University of Hawaii Press, Honolulu,
pp. 151–78.

Zang Rong (2000), 'Imperial Glass of the
Yongzheng Reign', *Elegance and Radiance:*

Bibliography

Grandeur in Qing Glass, The Andrew K. F. Lee Collection, Peter Y. K. Lam and Humphrey K. R. Hui (eds), Hong Kong: Art Museum, The Chinese University of Hong Kong, pp. 60–67.

Zhang Weiyong (2000), 'The Imperial Workshops of the Ming and Qing Dynasties and the Boshan Glass Works', *Elegance and Radiance: Grandeur in Qing Glass, The Andrew K. F. Lee Collection*, Peter Y. K. Lam and Humphrey K. R. Hui (eds), Hong Kong: Art Museum, The Chinese University of Hong Kong, pp. 76–7.

Zhao Rugua (1911), *Zhu fan shi. Chau Ju-kua: His Work on Chinese and Arab Trade in the Twelfth and Thirteenth Centuries, Entitled Chu-Fan-chi* [*Description of the Barbarous Peoples*], translated from the Chinese and annotated by Friedrich Hirth and W. W. Rockhill, St Petersburg, Imperial Academy of Sciences.

Zhu Jiajin (1982), 'A Study of the manufacture of painted enamelware of the Qing Dynasty', *Gugong bowuyuan yuankan*, **3**, pp. 67–76.

Zu Yizun (1782), *Jingting rixia jiuwen kao*. [Beijing?]

Index